D1563144

Payroll Certification Guide

Summaries for Quick Study

DEE NELSON, CPP

PO Box 221974 Anchorage, Alaska 99522-1974
books@publicationconsultants.com—www.publicationconsultants.com

ISBN 978-1-59433-129-9

Library of Congress Catalog Card Number: 2010921583

Manufactured in the United States of America.

TABLE OF CONTENTS

CHAPTER 1

Employee and Employer Relationship

Employee vs. Independent contractor *(Form W-2 vs. Form 1099 Misc.)*

There are two ways to determine the status of a worker and how they will be treated on your records for payment.

Common Law Test

IRS relies on Common Law Test

Key concept: **CONTROL: The right to control what work will be done and how that work will be done.**

Key Control Factors

Behavioral control

» Instructions and direction of work being done

» Training

Financial control

» Business expenses reimbursed/un-reimbursed?

» Substantial investment

» Services available to public-does this person do this same job for other businesses?

» How worker is paid *(by the job?)*

» Profit or loss?

Type of relationship

»Written agreement / contract

»Employee type benefits provided?

»Term of relationship

»Services an important aspect of regular operations?

Reasonable Basis Test

Section 530 of Revenue Act of 1978—Certain workers may be treated as independent contractors and exempt from federal payroll tax laws.

»Consistent treatment is mandatory

»Is this typical for industry?

Form SS-8 Determination of Worker Status for Purposes of Federal Employment Taxes and Income Tax Withholding—IRS will make status determination for you.

Employment Status Determined By Law (IRC)

Statutory Employees *(4 categories)*—Do not meet common law test but treated as employees for Soc Sec, Medicare *(and sometimes FUTA)*.

»Agent drivers / commission drivers

»Full time life insurance salespersons

»Traveling or City salespersons

»Home workers

Statutory Non-employees *(2 categories)*—Treated as independent contractors.

NO FIT, Soc Sec, Medicare or FUTA.

Compensation must be directly related to sales NOT hours worked.

Written contract must exist—*(NOT ee for FIT, SS, Med, FUTA.)*

»Qualified real estate agents

»Direct sellers

Temporary Help Agency Employees

»Hired, screened, trained, and paid by agency

»Agency has sole right to hire & fire

»Agency responsible for compliance with all
Payroll, HR, Benefits requirements

Leased Employees
>Hired, trained, qualified for client by leasing company
>Company MAY have the right to
   −hire/fire
   −set wage level
   −supervise work
>Leasing company responsible for
   −withholding & employment taxes
   −administration & funding of benefits
>Most beneficial to small companies
>Employer could bear responsibility if leasing company not financially sound

Federal Wage Hour Law
FLSA regulates:
>Minimum wage
>Overtime pay
>Child labor
>Equal pay for covered employees
Administered by U.S. Dept. of Labor Wage & Hour Division

State Unemployment Insurance Laws
Employer/employee relationship MORE inclusive and making the determination on a state level can be different than on a federal level. Some factors used by states are based on the type of tax.
>Some states follow common law test *(under FUTA)*
>Some states follow **ABC** test:
   −Absence of control
   −Business is unusual and/or away
   −Customarily independent contractor

State Disability Insurance Laws
States that have SDI follow SUI law

Worker Misclassification—Enforcement & Penalties

IRS Penalties

Unintentional misclassification

» Not withholding FIT - tax assessed = 1.5% of wages paid

» Not withholding FIT AND failure to file information return with IRS—tax assessed = 3% of wages paid

» Not withholding SS/Med taxes—tax assessed = 20% of ee share *(NOTE: 100% of er share must be paid)*

» Not withholding SS/Med taxes AND failure to file information return—tax assessed = 40% of ee share *(NOTE: 100% of er share must be paid)*

Intentional misclassification

» Employer liable for 100% of FIT and 100% of employee & employer SS/Med taxes

(NOTE: employer also subject to other penalties for failure to file returns or remit taxes).

IRS Enforcement Efforts

1099 Matching Program looks for

» Employees receiving only ONE Form 1099

» Employees receiving Form 1099 and Form W-2 from the same employer

Employment Tax Examination program

» Targeted at employers who are known to misclassify workers.

Employment Tax Adjustment program
(NOTE: information is shared with states & locals)

Workers Classification Settlement program allows for the tax payer and the IRS to settle claims of misclassification early on in the administrative procedures.

» Reclassification results in back taxes & retroactive benefits

FLSA Complaints Filed With Dept Of Labor

75% of audits triggered by employee complaints

Proof Of Right To Work In U.S.

Immigration Reform & Control Act of 1986 *(IRCA)*
»Form I-9 Employment Eligibility Verification

»All new hires MUST show identity AND right to work in U.S.

»Form I-9 must be completed within 3 business days from date of hire

»**I-9 retention:** 3 years from date of hire OR 1 year after termination *(WHICHEVER IS LONGER)*

Penalties for knowingly hiring unauthorized aliens *(civil penalties)*
»1st offense - $250 - $2000 for each worker

»2nd offense - $2000 - $5000 for each worker

»More than 2 offenses - $3000 - $10,000 for each worker

Penalty for failure to comply with verification requirements
»$100 - $1000 per worker

Repeated violations *(criminal penalties)*
»Up to $3000 and/or 6 months in jail

New Hire Reporting
Facilitates collection of child support

Uncovers fraud & abuse
»Unemployment compensation

»Workers compensation

»Public assistance *(welfare)* programs

Personal Responsibility and Work Opportunity Reconciliation Act of 1996 made way for the new hire reporting requirements.

New hire reporting began 10/1/1997

Reporting requirements
»Employee name, address, SSN

»Employer name, address, EIN

Reported to state

(NOTE: multistate employers can designate one state with approval from Secretary of Health & Human Services.)

Penalties

Civil penalties set by state

  » Up to $25 per occurrence

  » Maximum $500 if failure is willful *(conspiracy between ee & er)*

FLSA

The Fair Labor Standards Act

The Fair Labor Standards Act was enacted in 1938 and was also called the Wages and Hours Bill.

The FLSA regulates minimum wage rates, overtime pay, child labor, and equal pay for employees covered by the law. However, it also contains special rules for specific industries and situations.

Not all employees of covered businesses or who work in interstate commerce are entitled to the protections of the FLSA.

When human resources and payroll staff members speak of an "exempt" or "nonexempt" employee, they are referring to the employee's status under the FLSA.

Exempt employees are those who do not have to be paid the required minimum wage or overtime payments, and the employer does not have to keep certain records detailing their work.

The most well-known of these exemptions is the "white collar exemption" for executive, administrative, professional, and outside sales employees, but there are also narrower exemptions that apply to retail and service establishment employees, hotel and restaurant employees, and others.

Nonexempt employees must be paid at least the minimum wage for all hours worked, and an overtime premium for hours worked over 40 in a workweek.

There are tests to ensure you are classifying these employees correctly.

The short test

To be an exempt administrative EE under FLSA's short test the following conditions must be met:

»The EE must be paid at least $455 ,

»On a salary basis

»The EE's primary duty must consist of performing office or non-manual work directly related to ER's management policies or general business operations

»The EE's work must require discretion and independent judgment

On the state and local government level, EE's who are NOT subject to state or local civil service laws are exempt from the FLSA if they are in ONE of these categories:

»Publicly elected official

»Persons selected by an elected official (members of staff, or directly supervised by the official

»Persons appointed by elected official to serve in policy making position

»Persons who are immediate advisors of elected official

»Person employed by a state or local legislative branch, other than a legislative library or school board

If a certain situation is not covered by the FLSA, individual state wage-hour laws could cover them. Check with state DOL regulations to ensure they are not covered.

What does the Federal Wage and Hour law not cover

»Paid Vacations

»Sick Days

»Jury Duty Leave,

»Holiday,

»Lunch Breaks

»Coffee Breaks

»Equal Pay For Equal Work?

Walsh-Healy Public Contract Act

Passed in 1936 as part of the New Deal it protects employees who operate under government contracts over $10,000. The act also provides standards for minimum wage under the prevailing wage standard and establishes work rules for such employees to include OT, minimum wage and child labor laws.

Davis-Bacon Act

Passed in 1931 to established requirements for prevailing wage on public works projects. These projects include all construction contracts that are state or federally funded. The act also provides for standards for minimum wage under the prevailing wage standard as well as benefits due and work rules including OT and labor laws.

The minimum age required to work at the following positions under the FLSA:

»Railroad porter—18

»Gas station Attendant—14

»Fast food employee—14

»Grocery store clerk—14

»Vet technician—16

»Grocery store employee in the meat department—18

Many states have child labor laws that are more restrictive than the FLSA with regard to what jobs minors can do and what hours they can work. ER's should comply with the more restrictive law when covered by both federal and state law.

ER's can be fined, and/or the officers jailed, for their unlawful acts in violation of the FLSA.

»ER's that repeatedly or willfully violate the minimum wage and overtime provision of the law can be fined up to $1,000 for EACH violation.

»Child labor violations can bring fines of up to $11,000 for each violation that causes the death or serious injury of a minor.

»ER's that willfully violate the FLSA can be fined and/or the officers imprisoned for up to 6 months for second and later offenses.

The FLSA contains an exemption to the workweek standard for hospitals and nursing homes that is designed to give them more flexibility in scheduling. The law allows them to use a 14-day period, rather than a workweek, for determining overtime compensation. The following conditions must be met for the hospital and nursing home exemption to apply.

»There must be an agreement or understanding between the ER and the EE's before work is performed that the 14-day will be used.

» The agreement or understanding does not have to be in writing, but the ER must keep some special record of it.

» The ER must pay EE's covered by the agreement or understanding at least 1 ½ times their regular rate of pay for all hours worked over 8 in a day, or 80 in the 14-day period, whichever would result in higher pay for the EE.

CHAPTER 3

Taxable and Non Taxable

Personal Use of Company Vehicles

Commuting Valuation

Allows employer to value employee's personal use as $1.50 one way or $3 daily for commuting with company-owned auto under certain conditions (owned/leased by business, required to drive auto, written policy against further personal use, not a control employee) Limits change annually.

Annual Lease Valuation

FMV is determined by multiplying percentage of personal miles driven by annual lease value from IRS table. Fuel is not included, so must add actual cost or at annual limit set by the IRS. Can be prorated for months

Company Fleet Valuation

If at least 20 vehicles, employer can use the average fair market value of all vehicles with some restrictions

Vehicle Cents-Per-Mile Method

FMV of personal use is determined by multiplying the IRS standard business mileage rate set annually by IRS times the number of personal miles driven. There are restrictions on the use of this method. (Expect to drive at least 10,000 miles/yr, FMV cannot exceed annual limit set by IRS, and if the employee pays for fuel reduce by annual limit set by IRS per mile).

Record Keeping

Is Essential to Determine Business Vs. Personal Miles

Personal Use of Company Aircraft

The value of employee business travel in a company-owned airplane or helicopter is excluded from the EE's income as a working condition fringe benefit. But if travel is primarily personal, the value is included in the EE's income. Travel that combines business and personal purposes must be allocated to each. The value of EE's personal air travel can be determined by either the general valuation rule or the non-commercial flight valuation rule (flights on commercial aircraft are governed by different rules.)

> »**General Valuation Rule:** The value of personal flight on an employer provided aircraft (with pilot provided) would be allocated to EE. If more than one EE is on the flight, the value is allocated among them. If the ER does not provide the pilot, the value would be the amount paid to lease a comparable aircraft for the same time in the same area.

> »**Non-Commercial flight valuation rule:** The value of a personal flight where the employer provides the aircraft and the pilot is calculated by using an aircraft multiple based on weight of the aircraft and a cents-per-mile rate known as Standard Industry Fare Level (SIFL x mileage x aircraft multiple) + terminal charge = Value

Discount on Property or Service

EE discounts on goods or services normally sold to customers that do not qualify for the exclusion must be included in the employees income *(Real estate for any purpose, Stocks, bonds, currency, sales on services that exceed 20% of the sale price to customers, etc)*

Club Membership

Can be booked as working condition fringe (not taxable to employee) if there was a business purpose for some part and the employee substantiates expenses or employer does not include total cost as wages. Specific types of clubs may be exempt from this rule (business, trade, professional, etc)

Group Term Life Insurance

Calculate this cost given the age, amount of coverage, and cost from the Uniform Premiums IRS table. The taxable portion is the value of coverage over $50,000 minus any amount the employee paid for the coverage with after tax dollars. Taxable for SS and MED only. Exempt from FUTA and FIT withholding. The taxable value is posted to boxes 1, 3 & 5 and the Code "C" in Box 12 of the W-2. Employers can choose to withhold FIT

The Only EXEMPT GTL

Is when the beneficiary is employer, charitable organization or employee terminates during the year due to PERMANENT disability.

Nondiscrimination Testing Must Be Done On GTL Plan

Tax favored status is lost on values of coverage less than $50,000 if the plan favors Key employees The GTL plan is NOT Discriminatory if ONE of the following is met.

>70% of all employees benefit from plan

>85% participating employees are not Key employees

>All participants are part of a group classified as nondiscriminatory by IRS or

>The plan is part of a qualified cafeteria plan

Testing

>Corporate officer earning over annual limit set by IRS, limited to 50 officers, but in company with less than 500 employees, no more than 10% (but no less than 3 employees) may be treated as officers

>5% owners; OR

>1% owners whose annual earnings are greater than limit set by IRS annually.

Former Employees

Retirees who have taxable GTL have the uncollected SS and MED taxes shown in Box 12 with Codes "M" and "N".

Dependent GTL

Value of coverage up to $2,000 is not taxable income. If value is over $2,000, the entire amount becomes taxable income and must be computed using dependents age and IRS table (if age is not known, use employee's age). The taxable portion is subject to SS, MED, and FIT.

Whole Life Insurance or Straight Life Individual Insurance Policies

For key employees can be purchased by the employer or the premiums

17

on the policies already owned by the employees as an added benefit. Usually provide Death benefits *(equal to the face amount of policy)* and Savings *(portion of each premium is applied toward the savings segment of policy)*. As premium is paid the "cash surrender value" increases.

Straight Life Policies

If the proceeds of the policy are payable to the employee's designated beneficiary; the value of the policy that is paid for by the employer is included in income and subject to FIT. If the EMPLOYER is the beneficiary of the policy or the employee pays the premiums with AFTER-TAX dollars, the value of the policy is not included in income. If the insurance coverage is part of a plan intended to benefit employees/dependents, the value of the policy is NOT subject to SS, MED or FUTA tax.

Split Dollar Policy

Shared premiums by the employee and employer. The employer pays the annual increase in the cash value of the policy and the employee pays the remainder. At death the employer will receive the cash surrender value and the beneficiary receives the balance. The taxable benefit amount would be the employer-paid portion. The benefit amount is taxable for FIT but not SS, MED or FUTA

Moving Expenses

ONLY TWO deductible moving expenses

» Transportation of household goods

» In-transit storage of household goods and personal effects, and traveling from the old residence to the new **(lodging NOT meals)**

Any Nonqualified Expenses Report and Taxable for Ss, Med, FUTA, and FIT

Initial Tests of Deductibility

Before any expenses of a job-related move can be considered deductible and reimbursements for them excluded from income, TWO tests MUST be met:

» **Distance**—at least 50 miles farther from EE's old residence

» **Time**—during the 12 month period immediately following the move, the EE must work full-time for at least 39 weeks in the general location of the new workplace

Qualified Moving Expenses

Posted in Box 12, Code "P" of the W-2 (if paid to the employee). Any qualified moving expenses paid directly to a third party by the employer or any in-kind expenses provided are not reported at all on the W-2 as of 1998. Any nonqualified expenses report and taxable for SS, MED, FUTA, and FIT.

Educational Assistance

Currently JOB RELATED education is excluded taxable income as a working condition fringe if:

> »Necessary for minimum education requirement of job
>
> »Not taken to qualify for new job, and
>
> »Must be related to current job and help maintain
> or improve skill required by that job

Non-Job Related

Non-taxable for the first $5,250 annually addressed by IRS. Under Section 127, the educational assistance must be provided through an employer assistance program (EAP).

> »Undergraduate cpirsses, the income exclusion is now extended
>
> »Graduate courses ar INCLUDED in the exclusion
> for courses beginning after 12/31/01

Group Legal Services

Subject to SS, MED, FIT, and FUTA since exemption expired on 6/30/92

Employee Business Travel Expense Reimbursements

> »**Accountable**—reimbursements are not
> subject to reporting or taxation
>
> »**Non-accountable**—reimbursements are subject
> to SS, MED, FIT, and FUTA

Accountable plan MUST require

> »Business connection for expenses
>
> »Substantiation of expense within reasonable time
>
> »Return of any excess advanced amounts

If an EE fails to meet requirements of the accountable plan, only their expenses become taxable for SS, MED, FIT and FUTA

Watch out for continuing or permanent advances (impress funds) if EE's are given a fixed amount and later reimbursed after each trip for expenses—this type of plan would not be considered Accountable since amounts are not reasonably calculated to match expenses nor is the excess advance required to be returned.

In lieu of requiring EE's to substantiate expenses, employers can provide reimbursements in the form of a per diem allowance for each day traveled. There is no taxable income generated as long as the employee substantiates the time, place, and business purpose of travel as long as the per diem is at or below the federal per diem rate.

The IRS allows the use of a high-low per diem rate instead of the individual city rates if allowance is lodging, meals, and incidentals combined.

Mileage Allowances

ER's can reimburse EE's for travel away from home by mileage allowance. This only requires substantiation of the time, place, and business purpose. If the amount is not over the Federal limit that changes annually it is not taxable, anything over the Federal limit is taxable, reported in Box 12, Code "L" of the W-2 and is subject to SS, MED, FIT, FUTA.

The type of plan determines when to book the taxable portions of an EE's reimbursement. If the amounts are from an accountable plan but the EE fails to adhere to the rules, the taxable amount is booked on the next payday after the reasonable time has elapsed. If the amounts are from a non-accountable plan, the taxable income must be booked at the time of the disbursement.

Spousal Travel Expense

The ER can exclude the spousal travel expense payments from the EE's income IF the EE can show there was a legitimate business purpose and they substantiate the expense. IF they cannot do this, the expense becomes fully taxable.

ER Provided Meals

Generally the value of meals is excluded from the EE's income if:

» Furnished on the company premises

» For the convenience of the employer

ER Provided Lodging

The value of lodging can be excluded in the same rules as the meals and additionally the lodging is a condition of employment. The exclusion does not apply to either meals or lodging if a cash allowance is given instead of an "in-kind", or if the EE has an option to receive the cash or "in-kind" benefit.

Adoption Assistance

Allows an ER to provide up to annual limit set by IRS per eligible child (including special needs children) to cover adoption expenses. The qualified expenses include reasonable and necessary adoption fees, court cost, attorney fees, travel expenses (including meals and lodging) and other expenses related to the legal adoption of an eligible child. NON-qualified expense includes such expenses that are in violation of federal or state law, surrogate parenting arrangement, or in connection with the adoption of a child of the EE's spouse. The qualified expenses are NOT FIT taxed, but are subject to SS, MED, and FUTA. Reported in boxes 3, 5 and 12, code "T" on the W-2. All non-qualified expenses are fully taxable.

Advances and Overpayments

Fully taxable at time of distribution. If repaid in the same year, exclude amount from income and refund taxes regardless of when the repayment occurs in the year.

Awards and Prizes

Generally, fully taxable at the time of distribution. **IF CASH, ALWAYS TAXABLE**. If non-cash is given for length of service (min of 5 years) or safety achievement are excluded from income. Non-cash items to salespeople (paid solely commission) are NOT subject to FIT but is taxable for SS, MED, and FUTA.

Back Pay Awards

Generally if an EE wins a lawsuit for amounts other than personal injury or sickness, the award is considered back pay and is fully taxable. Other amounts awarded for fees, etc, are NOT taxable income. The back pay is generally treated as paid in the year of distribution, and not when "earned"; therefore report on current 941 and W-2. SSA has special rules about back pay awarded under a statute *(they credit back to year "earned")* therefore, special reporting is required to SSA *(see publication 957)*.

Bonuses

All bonuses paid in addition to regular wages are fully taxable at the time of distribution. Federal tax is at a flat rate of 25% starting in 2000.

Commissions

Amounts paid as commission on sales of goods or insurance are fully taxable at the time of distribution. The only EXCEPTION is a person paid strictly by commission; such payments would be FUTA EXEMPT.

Death Benefits

The Small Business Job Protection Act of 1996 repealed the income exclusion for up to $5,000 in death benefits to an employee's beneficiaries. These types of payments should be reported on a 1099R *(not subject to SS/MED).*

Dependent Assistance Programs

If employer has a valid written plan for dependent care, up to $5,000 annually can be excluded from FIT *($2,500 if married and filing separately).* Expenses are treated as incurred when the care is provided, not when payment is made. The benefit is reported in box 10 of the W-2 with any excess amounts being fully taxable.

Director's fees

Fees paid to non-employee directors of a corporation are not wages. They are reported on form 1099-MISC

Dismissal Pay

Severance pay is fully taxable at the time of payment.

ER Paid taxes (grossing up)

When an employer pays taxes that are normally EE withheld taxes, these amounts become taxable income to the EE. To calculate the proper taxes and taxable income, you must use the IRS approved "grossing up" formula: Gross amount = Desired net pay divided by the tax % minus 100%. The only other option for the EE is to have the taxes paid by the ER by "loaning" the tax funds to the EE. Amounts must be repaid by April 1st of the following year.

Equipment Allowance

If ER pays allowance to EE's who use their own tools and equipment, the allowance is not taxable income to the EE—Must segregate from regular wages—AND—cannot pay if tools/equipment are not being used.

Gifts

ALL gifts must be included as taxable income and fully taxable at the time of distribution. The only exception is if they can be termed deminimis... CASH IS ALWAYS taxable!

Golden Parachute Payments

Special rules by IRS allow key executives to receive payments after the change of corporate ownership up to three times the average compensation during the last five years. The entire parachute payment is subject to SS/MED and FIT, excess amount are also subject to 20% excise tax. These payments are reported in Box 12, Code "K" on the W-2.

Guaranteed Wage Payments

Some industries have guaranteed wages even if there is no work. These payments are fully taxable

Jury Duty Pay

The taxation depends on the policy of the ER.

»If EE receives regular wages in addition to jury duty pay from the court, the wages are fully taxable.

»If ER pays the difference between regular and jury pay, only the difference is fully taxable.

»If the ER pays regular wages, but requires the EE to sign over the jury duty check, again, only the difference is considered fully taxable. Then the EE can deduct jury pay on the 1040.

Leave Sharing Plans

If ER has leave banks, wages that are paid to EE are fully taxable, and the EE who donates the leave cannot deduct compensation from their income.

Loans to EE

If interest rates are below federal interest rates, the difference between federal rate and actual rate charged must be included as income, and fully taxed, if the loan is $10,000 or more on any one given day. However, FIT is not required to be withheld. If the loan is not paid back, the entire balance becomes fully taxable. When salespeople have draws against earned commissions, the amount is considered wages and fully taxable, unless they are being treated as a loan or advance in which case the payments can be exempt from tax under the compensation related loan rules.

Military Pay

Supplemental pay is governed by situation:

» Temporary assignment with National Guard or Reserves is fully taxable and report on the W-2

» If active duty or indefinite assignment, employment is broken so any compensation paid is not taxable and should be report on form 1099-MISC.

» Combat zone pay—*(or hospitalized as a result)* EXCLUDED from income with certain limitations.

–Afghanistan, including the airspace above, has been a combat zone since September 19th, 2001. The tax relief applies to US military and support personnel involved in operations in Afghanistan *(and Iraq starting 2006)*.

Outplacement Services

Amounts paid to former EE's to help them find a new job are exempt from taxes if:

» Business does not benefit

» EE does not have choice of cash or benefit

» EE would normally be able to deduct expenses on their 1040 return

Retroactive Wage Payments

Treated just as regular pay, fully taxable.

Security provided to EE's

The working condition fringe benefit rules apply if security is provided in a legitimate business situation (includes chauffeurs and body guards). If used for personal reasons, it would be fully taxable.

Stocks and Stock Options

If EE is paid stock in lieu of cash for compensation, the fair market value when transferred to the EE without restrictions is fully taxable wages. Incentive stock options (fixed price for specific time) are received, then it does not become taxable until the stock is sold and only under special circumstances. EE regular stock purchased at a discount has similar rules to avoid taxation at time of purchase. Non-qualified restrictions of discrimination. When ER must withhold taxes, the wages should be treated as supplemental wages.

Strike Benefits

Strike and lockout benefits paid by union to members are NOT wages. However, if they are paid hourly to picket, they are considered wages.

Tips

Generally all tips are fully taxable. If tips are deemed "service charge" and automatically billed to customer, the amount is treated as regular wages. EE must report tips if he/she receives more than $20/month. The tips are booked when they are reported to the ER, which should be by the 10th of the following month.

There are special rules for the ER share of FICA on unreported/underreported tips. The IRS has the ability to audit restaurants to prove EE reporting of all tips. If discrepancies are found, the ER is liable only for the ER's share of FICA and the EE is liable for the EE share.

Business Tax Credit for Tips

OBRA'93 allows restaurants a credit on their business return in an amount equal to the FICA tax paid on wages in excess of minimum wage. Form 8846 is used to report this credit.

Allocated Tips

If food and beverage businesses employ 10 or more EE's they must "allocate" tips if the amount of tips reported by employees is less than 8% of the establishments' gross sales subject to tips for that period. The difference between the amount reported by EE and the 8% must be allocated to the EE's and reported on the W-2 in box 8.

Uniform Allowance

If ER pays for cost of maintaining uniform through an advance or reimbursement, it is not taxable if it is required as a condition of employment and cannot be worn as normal street clothes.

Vacation Pay

Fully taxable, treated like regular wages even if no time off is taken.

Wages Paid After Death

If paycheck has been issued but not cashed, ER should reissue to appropriate person with all taxation the same. If the wages are paid after death in the SAME year, they are FIT exempt only. Report SS/MED on the W-2 but report the FIT amount on Form 1099 MISC (Box3). Wages paid the year following the death are reported on form 1099 MISC (box 3) and no taxes are withheld at the time of disbursement.

Any Cash Benefit

Is reported and taxed at the time of distribution.

Non-Cash Fringe Benefits

Are not required to be reported at any time other than by the end of the tax year (except investments and real property). Whenever they are posted or recognized as a benefit, taxes must be withheld, paid, and reported on the current 941.

Special Accounting Rules

IRS allows certain non-cash benefits provided in November and December to be reported in the following year. Both EE and ER must use the special accounting rule for reporting income/expenses.

CHAPTER 4

Benefit Taxation and Reporting

Health Insurance

Types of insurance

» Traditional—fee for service (most freedom to EE)

» HMOs

» Traditional HMO facility with docs, patients go to facility

» IPA (Individual Practice Association) physicians join group, patients go to member doctors

» PPOs (Preferred Provider Organization) patients receive higher level of benefits (lower cost) if they use a participating doctor

Tax Treatment

Generally ER contributions for accident/health plan benefits NOT wages subject to FIT, OASDI, Med, FUTA EE contributions

» If no Sec 125—contributions/deductions are from after tax wages

» If Sec 125 (salary reduction plan)—deductions from pre tax wages where allowed

» Benefits received not included in income if for **medical care defined by IRS**: *diagnosis, cure, mitigation, treatment or prevention of disease, or for the purpose of affecting any structure or function of the body*

» Plastic Surgery is NOT medical care.

» Employer paid physical exams NOT working condition fringe they are ER paid medical care expense.

Nondiscrimination
»Not required if thru 3rd party insurance company,
self insured—may not discriminate with benefits
or eligibility no matter who administers.

»Excess reimbursements are taxable.

»ADD payments for permanent loss NOT taxable wages.

Medical Savings Accounts

MSAs AKA Archer MSAs
Available ONLY with high deductible health insurance plan (individual coverage limit set annually).

For Family coverage, the plan must provide that no benefits are payable, no matter which family member incurs expenses, until the family as a whole incurs medical expenses exceeding annual limit.

Out of pocket expenses included deductibles, co-pays, and other amounts EE must pay for covered benefits, BUT NOT PREMIUMS.

ER contributions not included in income. EE contributions tax deductible (tax deduction on personal income tax).

Either ER or EE can make contributions NOT BOTH. Cannot be part of cafeteria plan (can exist outside of plan).

Tax treatment for earnings & distributions
»Earnings on MSAs not income until distributed

»Distributions excluded from income if for medical expenses
by covered member; cannot be used for premiums
except: long term care, COBRA continuation coverage;
premiums while receiving unemployment benefits

Reporting
»ER: W-2, Box 12, Code R

»EE: Personal income tax return

Long Term Care Insurance—HIPAA 1996
Beginning 1998 treated as accident & health insurance contracts. Amounts received EXCLUDED from income as received for personal injuries/sickness and reimbursements for medical expenses...if contract makes per diem pmts, the income exclusion is capped at annual limit set by IRS.

ER provided coverage excluded from income with the following

restrictions:
> »Not subject to COBRA continuation,

> »Not qualified benefit that can be offered as part of Sec 125 cafeteria plan,

> »Included in income if provided as part of flex spending arrangement.

COBRA Health Insurance Continuation (*Consolidated Omnibus Budget Reconciliation Act 1985*)

20 EE's, provide opportunity to elect continued group coverage for 18-36 months dependent on qualifying event.

Coverage must be the same. Qualified Beneficiaries entitled to coverage (spouse, dependents)

Qualifying events that result in loss of group health coverage:

> »Death of covered employee;

> »EE termination or reduction in hours (EXCEPT gross misconduct);

> »Divorce or separation;

> »Medicare entitlement;

> »Dependent child losing dep child status;

> »Bankruptcy proceeding

Period of Coverage:
> »Term or reductions in hours > 18 month (could be extended to a max of 36 month by another qualifying event);

> »ER bankruptcy, death of retiree > 36 month from death of EE; term/ reduction & qualified beneficiary is disable under SSA during first 60 days of continued coverage > 29 month for all qualified beneficiaries (could be extended to a max of 36 month by another qualifying event);

> »Death, divorce, separation, entitlement to Medicare, loss of dep child status > 36 mo.

Election & Notice Provisions
Coverage must be 'elected'. Election period at least 60 days beginning with date of coverage termination. Must provide written notice of COBRA rights to EE, notify plan administrator within 30 days of death, term, reduction, Medicare entitlement; notify plan administration within 60 days for divorce, separation, loss of dep child status; notify within 60 days if disabled under SSA or within 30 days if no longer disabled; plan administrator has 14 days to

notify qualifying beneficiaries of continual coverage rights after being notified of qualifying event.

Penalties for noncompliance

Tax of $100/day for each qualifying beneficiary (Max $200/day per family). Tax not imposed if reasonable cause and can be corrected within 30 days. Unintentional: max penalty during taxable year is LESSER of 10% of amount paid by ER during preceding year or $500,000.

Family and Medical Leave Act

Guarantees EE's workplace (50 EE's)12 weeks of unpaid leave in a year for:

»Newborn or newly adopted child;

»Care for seriously ill child, spouse, parent, self.

Guarantee continuation of EE health benefits while on leave.

LOOPHOLE: fewer than 50 EE's / worksite and > 75 miles between worksites.

Eligibility

EE for at least 12 month (consecutive not required) AND at least 1250 hours in the previous 12 month period. Expatriates not covered—must work within US, territory, or possession.

Serious Health Condition defined

Inpatient care or continuing treatment (incapacitated for 3 consecutive days) including subsequent treatment or medical supervision. Exceptions to continuing treatment: chronic conditions (asthma, diabetes, etc); pregnancy/prenatal care.

Intermittent leave allowed

Hours, days, weeks—note: reduced hours may be deducted from exempt EE salary.

Paid/Unpaid

ER can require eligible EE to use paid leave as part of 12 week guaranteed leave; must make known to EE (IN WRITING) within 2 business days of EE notice.

Health insurance benefits continue during leave

ER may require payments; 15 day notification required of intent to end coverage for non-payment. If EE does not return after FMLA, ER may recover premiums paid during leave. "return to work" = at least 30 days.

Job Guarantee
Previous job or equivalent—no loss of pay or benefits—seniority does not accrue during leave. KEY EE may be denied reinstatement if necessary to prevent economic injury to operations.

Recordkeeping
Basic PR records regarding hours worked, rate of pay, deductions, dates & amounts of FMLA leave including notices & docs related to FMLA.

Enforcement
FMLA administered by DOL, Wage & Hr Div.

Sick Pay

Purpose to replace wages due to illness or injury. Tax Treatment: depends on who makes pmts, who bears insurance risk; who paid premium; & whether temp or perm unable to work. WC is different—job related injury or illness.

Sick Leave Pay & Taxation

Regular pay received for brief absences due to illness or injury—subject to all taxes *(FIT, OASDI, Medicare, FUTA)*.

Sick Pay Under Separate Plan

»STD or LTD –pmts by ER, agent, or 3rd Party

»Taxation depends on how funded—if EE contributions after tax—benefits are not taxable income—if ER contributions or EE pre-tax contributions taxable income may be subject to FIT, OASDI, Medicare, FUTA—if ER & EE pay for disability plan, taxable income is attributed to ER portion of benefit.

»**Payments by ER**—ER must withhold FIT and < 6 month OASDI, Medicare, FUTA; > 6 month FIT only

Payments by agent
Treated as if made by ER, may be treated as supplemental wages, ER responsible for ER OASDI, Medicare, and FUTA unless agreement exists.

Payments by 3rd Party
If premium paid then 3rd party bears risk. 3rd party NOT required to withhold FIT unless requested by EE on W4S. 3rd party must withhold EE OASDI & Medicare < 6 month and MAY be responsible for ER OASDI &Medicare liability.

W-2 reporting

ER prepares W-2 either separate or combined, nontaxable sick pay Box 12 Code J.

Permanent Disability Benefits

Permanent= not expected to return to work; payments subject to FIT (if premium paid by ER or EE with pre-tax $ is exempt from OASDI & Medicare but not FUTA.

Workers Compensation

WC Benefit Payments

Not included in gross income—no employment taxes if paid under fed, state, or local law—excess ER payments fully taxable.

WC Premium Payment

Based on size of PR & risk codes for occupation within your business classification.

Exception classification codes:

  » Office workers

  » Outside sales

  » Drivers

WC payroll exclusions:

  » Overtime premium portion;

  » Reimbursed travel expenses;

  » 3rd party sick pmt;

  » Reimbursed moving expenses;

  » Tips;

  » Personal use of co. vehicle;

  » GTL > $50k;

  » Severance;

  » Educational assistance

Cafeteria Plans

Specific type of flex benefit plan under Sec 125 of IRC.

Benefits offered
Choice amount taxable (cash) and on-taxable (qualified)—must contain one of each.

Qualified non-taxable benefits not included in EE wages under IRC.
(ex: accident & health plans, medical, dental, vision, sick, dependent care, qualified adoption assistance, GTL)

Premium only plans (POPs)
Do not offer menu; allow EE pretax contributions toward premium.

Deferred Comp prohibited in cafeteria plans *(cannot carryover from one plan year to another)*—EXCEPTION: IRC Sec 401k for EE contributions and ER matching contributions.

Special rule for purchased vacation days
Purchased with pretax $; taxed when taken; restrictions: no carryover, cannot cash out after plan year end; may not use first—must use regular vacation first then purchased vacation.

Cafeteria Plan Funding
Either or both of the following:

> »Flex dollars/Flex credits—each EE receives
> specified amount to 'buy' selections

> »Salary reduction—EE salary used to purchase
> benefits thru pretax or after tax deductions

EE pretax benefit contributions *(AKA elective deferral / ER contribution)* result in higher take home pay.

Cafeteria Plan Document must be written; intention must be permanent.

Revocation of benefit elections
New elections or changes allowed only prior to beginning of plan year to remain in effect for plan year. Revocation or changes allowed for: change in marital status; change in dependent status; change in employment status, change in residence, adoption.

Special Exceptions:
> »COBRA, Medical support orders

> »Medicare/Medicaid eligibility, special
> enrollment rights under HIPAA

> »Elective deferrals under a CODA

> »FMLA leave changes.

Cost Driven Changes
If cost or coverage changes significantly EE may make change.

Cafeteria Plan Participation
Restricted to EE's and plan must be maintained for their benefit.

Nondiscrimination testing
Plan must not discriminate based on eligibility; contributions; or benefits in favor of highly compensated or key EE's.

Union Contract Exception
Exempt from nondiscrimination tests

Flex Spending Arrangements
EE saves pretax dollars—Coverage requirements: specified expenses reimbursed; maximum reimbursement cannot be substantially more than total premium.

Health Care Rules

»Elections cover full plan year;

»Uniform coverage throughout coverage period (plan year)

»Maximum funds must be available to EE at all time

»12 month period of coverage (plan year);

»Prohibited reimbursement- premium for ERs health plans;

»Claim substantiation:

−1. Statement/receipt AND

−2. EE statement that claim is not reimbursable

»Claims incurred during coverage period;

»Coordination with HIPAA requirements

Dependent Care Rules

»NO uniform coverage;

»Maximum $5000 / plan year;

»Coordination with dependent care tax

Tax Treatment of Cafeteria Plans

»ER contributions excluded from income, not subject to taxation if related to nontaxable benefits; EE pretax contributions.

»Excluded from income & not subject to taxation *(taxable benefits purchased are taxable when made available to EE)* EXCEPTION: 401k—no FIT, YES OASDI, Medicare, FUTA; EE after tax contributions—included in income; fully taxable; benefits purchased excluded from income;

»CASH instead of benefits purchased—wages fully taxable.

Discriminatory Plans discriminate in favor of highly comp EE's are not disqualified, but lose tax benefits of the plan—subject to tax *(states may differ)*.

Reporting Requirements

»**Pretax contributions** not on 941; not on W-2; YES on 940 *(Part I, Line 1 and Part I, Line 2)*; **taxable** fully reportable;

»**Cash or deferred arrangements** (401k) NOT FIT; YES OASDI, Medicare, FUTA; W-2 Boxes 3&5, 4&6, Box 12 Code D; 941 Lines 6a, 7a;

»**Dependent Care Assistance** *(FSA-dependent)* W-2 Box 10, any excess (>5000) Boxes 1, 3 5;

Form 5500
Suspended in 2002

Retirement & Deferred Compensation Plans
Qualified Pension & Profit Sharing Plans (Sec 401a).

»**Pension** benefit determined @ retirement, payable over #yr/EE life, ER contributions not tied to profits.

»**Profit Sharing** ER contributions based on formula tied to profits .

»**Defined benefit plans** provide specified level of benefits during EE retirement usually based on age, comp., length of service.

»**Payroll maintains records** hours worked, comp earned, DOB, DOH, for actuary/administrator.

»**Defined contribution plan** individual accounts for each EE; predefined amount contributed by ER and/ or EE; retirement benefit dependent on acct balance @ retirement *(Ex: money purchase pension plan—ER contributes annually based on EE comp for yr)*.

»**Profit Sharing** company/ER makes substantial/recurring contributions; amounts contributed invested for distribution @ retirement; ER contributions determined by formula-may or may not be tied to profits

» **Annual Compensation & Contribution Limits**—annual compensation limit is set annualy; limit also used in nondiscrim testing; annual contribution limit is set by IRS= TOTAL ER & EE contributions to defined contribution plan cannot exceed LESSER or annual limit set by IRS OR 100% of EE comp.

» **"Catch-up" Contributions**—At least 50 years old by the end of the plan year (If employee will reach 50 before the end of the calendar year, he/she is deemed 50 as of 1/1 of that year), can defer an additional amount set annually by the IRS. IMPORTANT—ALL catch-up plans had to be in place by October 1, 2002.

» **IMPORTANT**—The catch up contribution provision does not apply during a governmental 457(b) plan participant's last 3 years before retirement, when normal elective deferral limits are increased.

» **Tax treatment of pension & profit sharing plans**—ER contributions to qual plan excluded from wages & not taxed. Qual Plan: meet requirements of Sec 401a; participation, vesting, contrib. Limits, benefit limits, nondiscrim. EE after tax contributions included in income & fully taxable.

Payments/Benefits from Pension plans are taxable when received by EE/RetEE if attributed to ER contributions, investment gains, pretax deferred amounts. EE after tax contrib. are not taxed. Taxable pmts FIT only not OASDI, Medicare, and FUTA. 10% excise tax if distributed prior to age 59. Qualified annuity plans (Sec 403a) ER contributions not wages, not taxed.

Cash or Deferred Arrangements (401k–CODA)

Pretax (deferred comp) contrib. not subject to FIT until withdrawn

Qualified CODA must meet Sec 401k requirements, ER can make salary reductions without an election.

Contribution Limits Sec 401k

Limit set annually by IRS

Nondiscrimination testing
Must satisfy one of two tests—the actual deferral percentage (ADP) of eligible h.c. EE for the current plan yr cannot exceed the ADP of eligible non h.c. EE for preceding plan yr by more than certain amount—matching & after tax contrib. can be included.

Failure of ADP test

All participants will be taxed on elective deferrals unless plan takes corrective action.

Tax Treatment 401k plans

EE elective deferrals & ER match not wages subject to FIT, EE deferrals subject to OASDI, Medicare, FUTA; ER match not taxed.

Reporting requirements

W-2, not Box 1, Yes Box 3&5, Box 12 Code D, Box 13 check retirement plan; Excess deferrals Box 12 not Box 1, reported EE personal income tax form; For 941 not line 2, yes 6a, 7a; Form 940 Part I, Line 1.

Early distribution penalty

10% excise tax <59 ½, unless disabled, separated employment after age 55, receiving periodic distributions.

401k NOT for public sector groups

Veterans can make additional elective deferrals for time spent in military service; additional amounts not subject to limits.

Tax Sheltered Annuities (Sec 403b)

For public schools & tax exempt charitable, religious, educational organizations may not offer 401k unless existed prior to TRA of 1986. Automatic salary reductions can qualify as elective deferrals

Contribution Limits

Must have at least 15 years of service with ER but limited to the lesser of $3000 in additional contributions in any year, $15,000 reduced by any amounts contributed under this special provision in earlier years, or $5,000 multiplied by #of years of service minus total elective deferrals from previous years. Limit set annually.

Elective deferral limit is set annually by the IRS

Tax Treatment (403b)—EE elective deferral / ER contributions not FIT wages (up to limits)

Distributions taxable; EE deferral subject to OASDI, Medicare, FUTA; ER contributions not. Reporting requirements 403b—Form W-2 not Box 1, yes Boxes 3&5 and 4&6, Box 12 Code E, Box 13 check retirement box; Excess deferrals Box 12 not Box 1; Form 941 not line 2, yes 6a, 7a; Form 940 Part I, Line 1.

Individual Retirement Accounts

ER sponsored IRA must be in writing for benefit of EE's & must limit contributions to $3,000. EE contribution is deductible but the limit is reduced if EE or SPOUSE are active participants in any qualified retirement plan. Reduction based on age *(adjusted gross income)*.

Tax Treatment IRA included in income, not subject to FIT up to amount EE will be able to deduct; subject to OASDI, Medicare, and FUTA. Distributions taxable.

Simplified Employee Pensions (408k) SEP

SEP is an IRA that meets requirements governing EE participation, nondiscrimination, withdrawals, & written formulas to determine ER contribution. ER must make contribution on behalf of EE > age 21 have worked at least 3 of last 5 years and earned at least annual limit.

Salary reduction agreement—EE can elect to defer annual limit set by the IRS BUT at least 50% of eligible EE's MUST participate or no one can do it. Only available to ERs with <=25 EE's.

Tax Treatment SEP—ER contributions not taxable; excess ER contributions included in wages; EE deferrals subject to OASDI, Medicare, FUTA

Reporting SEP—ER contributions-NO; EE deferral Form W-2 no Box 1, yes Boxes 3&5, 4&6, Box 12 Code F, Box 13 check retirement plan; Form 941 no Line 2, yes 6a & 7a; Form 940 yes Part I, Line 1.

Employee Stock Ownership Plans (ESOP)

Invests in ER stock; meet requirements of Sec 401a for participation, vesting, nondiscrimination; ESOP buys stock with ER contributions or borrowed funds. **Tax treatment**—ER contributions not wages, not taxable; may not exceed LESSER of 100% EE annual comp set by the IRS.

Nonqualified Deferred Compensation Plans

Used for high level executives—no restrictions

Tax Treatment—ER contributions based on constructive receipt, taxable when set aside, accessible without restrictions. Can be funded or unfunded *(based on ER promise to pay)*; taxed when paid to EE; fully taxable.

CHAPTER 5

Payment of Wages

Pay Frequency

The timing of paychecks is usually determined by the state DOL. There are many pay periods that can be used and the employer can choose but must stay within the state mandated regulations. The things that the state regulates about pay periods are as follows:

>»State by State pay frequency requirements

>»Pay frequency required

>»Lag time before pay

Payment on Termination

The timing of when employees need to be paid upon termination depends on state law and by the method in which the employee leaves employment i.e. termination or resignation. The things that the state regulates about payments are as follows:

State by State wage payment requirements upon termination

Involuntary Resignation—days to be paid

Voluntary Resignation—days to be paid

Payment Methods

The way in which an employer pays the employee is also regulated by the state and the federal DOL.

Cash or Check

In general, employees must be able to cash their paychecks or other negotiable instruments provided by the employer for their face value without a charge or discount by a financial institution. Example: tokens or coupons, whatever form of payment is used, employees must be able to convert it to cash on payday.

Direct Deposit (electronic funds transfer)

Problems associated with employee paychecks:
» Lost or stolen

» Unclaimed or not cashed

» Time take for employee to cash check

» Storage of cancelled checks

» Early preparation of vacation checks

How the process works:
» Employee authorization

–Name

–Bank routing number

–Type of account (checking or savings)

–Account number

» Employer prepares an automated file of direct deposit

» File is sent to originating depository financial institution (ODFI)

» The file is then sent through the automated clearing house network (ACH)

» ACH provides delivery of the files to the receiving financial institution (RDFI)

» The RDFI posts the funds to the designated employees' accounts

Federal/State requirements:
Under federal rules, an employer may not make it a condition of employment that an employee has to accept direct deposit at a PARTICULAR financial institution. An employer CAN require an employee to accept direct deposit IF it gives the employee a CHOICE among financial institutions, or it CAN require an employee to choose between direct deposit at a particular financial institution or payment by check or cash.

Where state laws are more protective of employees (prohibiting compulsory direct deposit), they supersede federal law and regulations

Prenotifications—Optional as of September, 1996

Direct Deposit is not paperless:
　　»Authorization agreement (when written)

　　»Information statement (pay stub)

Cost and Benefits:
　　»Loss of float time

　　»Processing services

　　»Bank services charges

Pay Statements Provided To Employees

The way an employer provides pay information to an employee is also regulated by the state. Each state specifically outlines what information should be on the pay stub.

Unclaimed Paychecks

Unclaimed paychecks are handled in various ways and are state regulated. The process can be as follows:

　　»The unclaimed wages become "abandoned property"

　　»The employer must pay to the appropriate state agency (usually the treasury) if they remain unclaimed for a certain number of years. The State laws governing abandoned property are known as "ESCHEAT" laws, because the property "escheats" to the state.

Wages Owed

Most states also regulate wages owed to deceased employees, in terms of who the wages may be paid to, how much may be paid before administration of the deceased estate, and what conditions must be met.

CHAPTER 6

Withholding and Paying Taxes

Constructive Payment

This is actual payment. Considered to have been paid wages when the wages have been made available to the employee without "substantial limitation or restriction."

Employee is not required to have actual possession of the wages for the principle of constructive payment to apply. It is enough that the wages are available to be drawn on or controlled by the employee.

When the wages are made available to the employee in this manner, the employer must withhold required taxes.

Paychecks sent through the mail generally are not constructively paid when sent. The wages are not available to the EE until the check is delivered.

Regardless of the date that is printed on the EE's check, the date it is actually or constructively provided to the EE is the date that triggers the ER's withholding and deposit obligations.

Social Security Numbers

ER's use their EE's SSN's to identify them when reports of wages paid and taxes withheld are made to the SSA and the IRS.

ER's must get each new EE's name and SSN and enter them into its records EXACTLY as shown on the social security card.

Employers are required to verify SS# to Name through Social Security Administrations Employee Verification System.

May be photocopied but not color copied. Newly hired EE's who do not have an SSN can get one by filling out and submitting Form SS-5.

Verifying Social Security Numbers

Original social security card, telephone to SSA (up to 5 SSN's), paper list to SSA (up to 50 SSN's), or employee verification service (unlimited)

www.ssa.gov go to this web site for internet verification of SSN

For an employee name change, employer should refuse to make the change until a new SS card with the new name is presented.

Even if there is no withholding, exempt status employees must also produce a SSN for W-2 statements.

SSA sends Social Security Statements (SSS) to Employees

Mailed about 3 months before employees birthday to employees age 25 and over. EE may still request a SSS by filing form SSA-7004. The SSS reflects information provided on an EE's W-2.

Form W-4

Newly hired employees should complete Form W-4 on or before the first day of work. An amended W-4 submitted within 10 days

Exempt status in effect for 1 calendar year and requires a new W-4 by February 15th of the following year to keep the exempt status.

> » Had a right to a refund of all FIT withheld in the prior year because there was no liability

> » Expects to have no tax liability in the current year

> » Cannot be claimed as a dependent on someone else's income tax return if the EE's income will exceed $750 and will include more than $250 of non-wage income (dividends and interest) in 2004.

> » Employer has to notify employee by Dec 1 of the need to change status from exempt or more than 10 for new calendar year.

Form W-4 tells employer marital status, number of withholding allowances, claiming exempt, and additional dollar amount.

Withholding allowances:

> » 1 for EE *(unless being claimed as a dependent)*

> » 1 for EE's spouse *(unless working and claiming exemption for him/herself)*

> » 1 for each dependent *(other than spouse and only if spouse is not already claiming the dependent)*

> » 1 additional for spouse not working *(or single with one job)*

»1 for head of household

»Additional allowances based on employee's itemized deductions

Watch out for:

»Giving tax advice *(refrain from giving tax advice)*

»Students claiming exempt *(Must meet all the test for exemption—see above)*

»Nonresident aliens *(if claiming exempt, but also file new form every year)*

Reject a W-4 Form when unauthorized alterations or striking of any language—ER's are NOT responsible for verifying the accuracy of the information provided, ER's cannot knowingly accept an invalid W4.

»If current EE refuses to provide a valid W4, do not change the information, keep withholding according to the most recent valid W4

»If a new hire EE, withhold as if the EE were single with zero.

»If questionable, send a copy with a letter explaining why you are questioning the W4 to the IRS at: Fresno Customer Service Center, Questionable W4 Program, P.O. Box 24015, Mail Stop 813, Fresno, CA 93776. (withhold according to EE's instruction until/unless you hear from the IRS).

Flat dollar amount or straight percentage is invalid.

Do not take tax payments from employees.

Employers no longer have to submit a W-4 to the IRS when employee claims more than 10 withholding allowances, the employee claims exempt

Filing Form W-4 magnetically or electronically.

Successor employers keep the Forms W-4 by its former employees and new employees must fill out new forms

Retain the W4's for at least 4 years after the date the last return was filed using the information.

Form W-4P

Retirees can:

»Elect not to have any FIT withheld *(except for payments sent to US citizens or resident aliens outside the US).*

»Designate a certain number of withholding allowances to be used in calculating the amount withheld

»Indicate an additional dollar amount to be withheld

If W-4P is not submitted, ER's must withhold as if the EE is married claiming 3 withholding allowances.

Form W-4S

Sick pay paid by a third party insurer when an employee wants federal tax withheld.

Withhold a flat dollar amount, the minimum amount to be withheld is $20 per week. After withholding the EE must receive at least $10.

Methods of Withholding FIT

Whatever method is used, the basis for the calculation is the ER's payroll period, or frequency with which it pays its EE's.

Rounding is permitted—if used, must do it consistently.

Wage Bracket Method

Know what the EE is claiming, Married or Single and the number of allowances.

Locate the correct marital status and frequency table established annually by the IRS.

Determine wages subject to FIT

Locate wage bracket, if equal to a wage-bracket amount, use the next higher tax bracket

Move across the wage bracket amount until you find the column with the correct number of withholding allowances, this is the tax to be withheld

Is there additional dollars to be withheld, if yes, add this amount to the tax to be withheld.

Percentage Method

»Find number of withholding allowances on W-4

»Find value of allowance

»Determine the wages subject to federal income tax

»Subtract the value of allowance

»Locate the percentage method table single or married

»Add any extra dollar amount

Alternative Withholding Methods

Annualized wages
Based on annual payroll period and then divided among the actual payroll periods.

Cumulative wages
For wage payments that are consistently high and low

Part-year employment
Similar to cumulative wage method but reduces withholding for EE's who work only during part of the calendar y ear, usually on a seasonal basis or because they have been unemployed.

> »Must be requested in writing

> »No more than 245 days of continuous employment

> »Must be discontinued if the ER finds the EE will work
> more than 245 days during the calendar year.

Supplemental Wage Payments

Payments made to employees that are not considered earning for work performed are considered supplemental wages and need to be treated differently for tax and reporting purposes. Examples of such payments include:

> »Bonuses, prizes, and awards

> »Commissions

> »Back pay awards

> »Retroactive pay

> »Overtime pay

> »Severance

> »Tips

> »Payments for working during vacation

> »Reimbursements for nonqualified moving expenses

> »Reimbursements for business expenses under non accountable

Taxation of such payments is handled as follows:

> »Combine payments—if supplemental wages are combined
> with regular wages for a payroll period and the amount
> of each payment is not clearly indicated, the ER must
> withhold FIT as if the combined payment is a wage
> payment for that period *(regular withholding)*

> »Flat withholding rate—If supplemental wages are paid separately

from regular wages, or when combined but clearly indicated, the ER may withhold FIT at the rate of 25%, but ONLY if FIT was withheld from the last regular wage payment *(if claiming exempt, then these wages are also exempt)*

» Aggregate method—Must use if the EE has no FIT withheld from regular wages because the number of allowance claimed. The wages from the most recent payroll period is combined with the supplemental wages. After calculating the withholding on the total amount, using the wage-bracket or percentage method, the amount already withheld from the last wage payment is subtracted to reach the amount that MUST be withheld from the supplemental wage payment.

Withholding on Pensions and Annuities

Periodic payments made over a period of more than 1 year and recipients can use form W-4P

Non periodic payments of at least $200 are subject to 10% rate withholding or form W-4P.

Eligible rollover distributions 20% unless the distribution is directly rolled over to another qualified plan.

» EE can choose to receive part of a rollover and the balance rolled over directly to a qualified plan and only pays taxes and penalty on the amount actually received by EE. *(No withholding is required if the total of all payments is less than $200)*

Backup Withholding

Must withhold 28% if:

» Payee fails to provide the payer with a TIN

» The IRS notifies the payer that TIN is incorrect through a B notice

– If "B" notice is received, withholding must begin no later than the first payment after 30 days from receipt of the notice and will last until another TIN is properly furnished.

– Once "B" notice is received, the ER has 15 days to send a copy to the payee along with a W9 requesting correct information.

» The IRS notifies the payer that a payee has underreported interest or dividend payments

» The payer does not receive from a payee receiving interest or dividend payments a certification that the payee is not subject to withholding

Advance Earned Income Credit (EIC)

Earning limits apply and are adjusted annually by the IRS.

Eligible employees with no qualifying children:

»Must be at least 25 years of age, but no older than 65

»Live in the US for at least half the year

»Cannot be claimed as a dependant on someone else's tax return

»Non-resident aliens are NOT eligible

»Military personnel stationed outside the US are considered to be living in the US during that time

»Does NOT include wages earned as an inmate, work release, or halfway house.

»Individual who fraudulently claimed the EITC in an earlier year are NOT eligible to claim it for the next 10 years *(only 2 years if in error)* .

»Does NOT include payments made under a public assistance program

Advance EIC payments require a filed Form W-5

Invalid certificates—if incomplete, unsigned, altered in any way, if EE has orally or in writing indicated that the form is false. Consider them VOID.

Changed circumstances—EE must revoke it in writing within 10 days of the change.

Circular E tables—based on all compensation paid to EE for services rendered that are subject to FIT, marital status, and whether EE's spouse has a W5 in effect.

If EE has claimed exempt from withholding on W4, earned income is the wages that would have been subject to withholding without the exemption.

Social Security and Medicare Taxes

Social Security tax rate is 6.2% and the wage base is determined annually by the IRS, Medicare Tax rate is 1.45% on unlimited wages

Employees working for more than one employer have withholding from all employers

Rounding to the nearest dollar is not permitted

Self-employed individuals pay both shares of the tax

Wages exempt from Social Security and Medicare Taxes

Sickness or injury payments under workers' comp

Sick or disability benefits paid to or on behalf of an employee more than 6 calendar months after the last month the employee worked

Payments under a deferred compensation plan

Payments under a Section 125 flexible benefits plan

Noncash payments for work done outside the employer's trade

Types of Employment Exempt from Social Security and Medicare Taxes

Work done by temporary foreign agricultural workers

Work performed by a child under age 18 for his parents

Work on a foreign ship or aircraft outside the US by non-US citizens

State and Local Government Employees

All state and local government employees hired after 4/1/86 are covered by Medicare and must pay the tax

Other exemptions from this mandatory coverage

Penalties for Failure to Withhold

Employers liable for payment of federal income tax

The Internal Revenue Code focuses most of its penalties for employers on the failure either to deposit the proper amount of taxes on time or to file correct returns on time. Regarding withholding, the Code makes employers liable for payment of federal income tax deducted and withheld from employees' wages, while relieving employers of liability for the withheld amounts to anyone other than the federal government. Even though an employer fails to withhold federal income tax, if the employer can show the employee later paid the tax, the employer is no longer liable for the amount not withheld. However, this provision does not mean employers will not be faced with other penalties associated with the failure to withhold, such as late deposits or returns or the "responsible person" penalty Third-party liability. There are special rules governing penalties for third parties who supply funds to an employer for the purpose of paying wages to that employer's employees, knowing that the employer cannot or will not deposit the required withholding taxes. In such situations, the third party is liable for the amount of taxes not paid plus interest, up to a maximum of 25% of the funds supplied to pay wages. The 25% limitation is an absolute maximum for both taxes and interest owed. The time limit for the IRS to collect such taxes and interest is 10 years, although the parties may voluntarily agree to extend the time limit even further.

CHAPTER 7

Unemployment

Federal Unemployment Insurance

On the federal level, employer contributions in the form of unemployment taxes are required by the Federal Unemployment Tax Act (FUTA).

FUTA tax is paid only by employers and is calculated as a percentage of covered wages for each employee.

FUTA taxes cannot be withheld from employee's wages.

Who Must Pay FUTA Tax

Employers meeting one of the following criteria must pay federal unemployment tax:

»Nonfarm employers paying $1,500 or more in covered wages in any calendar quarter during the current or preceding calendar year;

»Nonfarm employers employing at least one employee for at least part of one day in 20 different weeks (not necessarily consecutive) during the current or preceding calendar year;

»Farm employers paying $20,000 or more in covered wages in any calendar quarter during the current or preceding calendar year;

»Farm employers employing at least 10 employees for at least part of one day in 20 different weeks (not necessarily consecutive) during the current or preceding calendar year; or

»Employers paying domestic employees $1,000 or more in any calendar quarter of the current or preceding calendar year for work performed in a private home, local college club, fraternity, or sorority.

Some employers are not covered despite meeting the above criteria:
»Federal, state, and local government employers, including
their political subdivisions, and Indian tribes; and

»Nonprofit religious, charitable, or educational
organizations that is tax-exempt.

What Wages Are Exempt from FUTA

In general, all employee compensation is subject to FUTA tax unless specifically exempted under the Internal Revenue Code. Following is a list of several exempt payments.

»Sick or disability benefits paid more than six calendar months
after the last month the employee worked for the employer;

»Sickness or injury payments made under a
state workers' compensation law;

»Payments made under a deferred compensation
plan, except elective deferrals to the plan;

»Payments made under a Section 125 flexible benefits
plan (i.e., cafeteria plan), other than elective
deferrals to a deferred compensation plan;

»The value of group-term life insurance coverage over $50,000;

»Wages paid to a beneficiary after the year of an employee's death

What Types of Employment Are Exempt from FUTA

In addition to the wage payments listed above, certain types of employment are also exempt from FUTA. Here is a list of some of them:

»Work performed for a federal, state, or local government
employer, including political subdivisions;

»Work on a foreign ship outside the U.S.;

»Work done by full-time students for the school where
they attend classes or for an organized camp;

»Work done for a foreign government or an international
organization *(e.g., NATO, the United Nations)*;

»Work performed as student nurses or hospital interns;

»Insurance agents who receive only commissions;

»Work performed by statutory nonemployees *(direct
sellers, newspaper deliverers, and real estate agents)*

FUTA Tax Rate and Wage Base

FUTA tax rates and wage base is determined annually by the IRS. Most employers do not pay the full 6.2%. If state unemployment taxes are paid in full and on time, employers can receive a credit against FUTA of up to 5.4%, for an effective rate of 0.8%.

Constructive payment rules apply. FUTA applies only when wages are actually or constructively paid, not when earned.

Employees working for more than one employer. Wage limit must be applied to wages paid by each employer; wages may not be aggregated.

Successor employers. If both the predecessor and the successor are covered employers under FUTA the successor employer can consider the wages paid to an employee by a predecessor company when determining the FUTA wage base.

Common paymaster. Related corporations can combine wages paid to concurrently employed employees by a common paymaster when determining the FUTA tax wage base.

Depositing and Paying FUTA Tax

Employers must determine their FUTA tax liability on a quarterly basis. At least for the first three calendar quarters of the year employers can assume they will be entitled to the full 5.4% credit for state unemployment insurance contributions. So, employers can calculate their FUTA liability by multiplying their FUTA taxable wages for the quarter by 0.8%.

In each of the first three quarters, if the employer owes more than $100, the full amount must be deposited by the last day of the month following the end of the quarter.

Extra day for weekends and holidays
If the FUTA tax deposit date falls on a Saturday, Sunday, or federal or state legal holiday, the deposit is due on the next business day.

Special rule for small amounts owed
No deposit is necessary when the employer's FUTA liability for a calendar quarter is $100 or less. The liability is carried over and added to the employer's liability for the next quarter.

Final quarter liability
Employers determine their fourth quarter FUTA liability when they complete Form 940, *Employer's Annual Federal Unemployment (FUTA) Tax Return* (or the short form, Form 940-EZ, if applicable). The employer determines

how much of the 5.4% state credit it is actually entitled to and how much its total FUTA balance for the year is.

If the total balance due (after taking into account previous deposits and any undeposited amounts from prior quarters) is more than $100, the full amount owed must be deposited by January 31.

If the balance due is $100 or less, payment can be attached to the employer's Form 940 or 940-EZ when the form is filed *(by January 31ˢᵗ)*.

Calculating the State Credits against FUTA Tax Liability

An employer's FUTA tax rate of 6.2% can be reduced by up to 5.4% through credits based on the amount and timeliness of state unemployment taxes paid.

There are two types of credit against FUTA liability, the "90%" or "normal" credit and the "additional" credit.

Normal credit

"90%" or "normal" credit. The normal credit provides a reduction in FUTA liability for payments <u>required</u> and <u>actually made</u> under state unemployment compensation laws. It is also called the 90% credit because the amount of the credit is limited to 90% of the basic 6.0% FUTA tax rate or 5.4%, *(the other 0.2% is surtax)*. Several requirements must be met before credit can be taken:

»Payment must be made by Form 940 due date.

   –To receive the full normal credit, all state unemployment taxes owed must be paid by the filing date for Form 940.

»State must have "certified" unemployment insurance program.

   –To qualify for the normal credit, the U.S. Department of Labor must certify the state law requiring payment of state unemployment taxes. The state must also make timely payments of all interest due on loans from the federal unemployment fund.

»Payments must be "required" by state law.

   –Voluntary contributions to reduce an employer's unemployment tax rate cannot be part of the normal credit. *(They may, however, contribute to the "additional" credit an employer gets when paying a state tax rate of less than 5.4 %.)*

»Amounts owed must "actually" be paid.

   –Cannot be held in separate accounts while challenging state tax rate assessments.

»State contributions must be paid by the employer.

–Several states require employees as well as employers to make unemployment contributions. Such employee contributions may not be taken as a credit against the employer's FUTA liability. But if the employer voluntarily pays the employees' share of state unemployment tax liability, it will receive normal credit for those payments.

Additional credit

The additional credit allows employers with lower unemployment tax rates to receive the same credit against FUTA tax liability as other employers. These lower rate employers are grated an additional credit equal to the difference between their tax rate and 5.4%. When added to the normal credit, the total credit cannot exceed 5.4%. The availability of the additional credit does not depend on the timeliness of the employer's state tax payments.

Successor employers

Successor employers acquiring predecessor companies that are not employers under FUTA when the acquisition is made receive a FUTA tax credit for state unemployment taxes paid by the predecessor that relate to employees who work for both the predecessor and the successor.

Credit reduction because of state loans

States with a high rate of unemployment can borrow money from the federal unemployment insurance fund to pay benefits. If a state's loan is not repaid within the specified time FUTA credits available for employers in that state are reduced. The extra FUTA taxes paid are applied against each state's loan balance.

Reporting FUTA Tax on Form 940

Employers covered by FUTA must report their liability <u>annually</u> on Form 940, *Employer's Annual Federal Unemployment (FUTA) Tax Return.*

Employers may pay their fourth quarter liability with Form 940 if the liability is $100 or less.

Form 940 determines the employer's FUTA taxable wages for the calendar year and the FUTA tax liability on those wages after accounting for applicable state unemployment tax credits and FUTA tax deposits made during the year.

Can you use Form 940-EZ?

The first three items on Form 940 (Questions A through C) are questions that determine if the employer is eligible to file Form 940-EZ, *Employer's Annual Federal Unemployment (FUTA) Tax Return.* An employer can file Form 940-EZ if:

»State unemployment taxes were paid to only one state;

» State unemployment taxes were paid by the
   due date of Form 940; and

» All the employer's FUTA taxable wages were also
   taxable for state unemployment taxes.

Employers in a credit reduction state cannot use Form 940-EZ. In years where at least one state is subject to credit reduction, a fourth question is added to the items appearing at the top of Form 940.

What companies must file Form 940?

Each employer covered by the Federal Unemployment Tax Act must file a Form 940 (or 940-EZ).

When there has been a sale of the business entity, only the wages paid by that employer should be reported.

If two companies merge or consolidate in a statutory merger, the entity that results is the employer that must file the Form 940, since it is now considered the same employer as the absorbed corporation. It must report the wages paid by both corporations. The first return it files after the merger must have a statement attached with the following information:

» The fact of the merger

» Date of the merger

» The absorbed corporation's name, address, and EIN

Even though a successor employer may be allowed to include wages paid by a predecessor company to employees of both companies when determining whether the FUTA wage base has been met, generally each company must file its own Form 940 for wages it paid. There is an exception where the successor acquires a predecessor that was not an employer covered by FUTA.

IRS provides the form.

By the end of the calendar year, employers that have filed Form 940 in the past will receive a new form from the IRS with a preprinted address label.

Form must have employer's signature.

The Form 940 must be signed by:

» The individual owning the business, if it is a sole proprietorship;

» The president, vice president, or other principal corporate
   officer, if the employer is a corporation;

»An authorized member or partner of an
  unincorporated association or partnership having
  knowledge of the organization's affairs; or

»A fiduciary if the employer is a trust or estate.

»Other individuals may sign the return as an agent of the
  employer or if they have a valid power of attorney.

When must Form 940 be filed?

Generally Form 940 (or 940-EZ) must be filed by January 31 of the year after the FUTA tax liability was incurred.

If January 31 is a Saturday, Sunday, federal or state holiday the form is due on the next business day.

Employers get an automatic extension to February 10 if they have deposited their FUTA tax liability in full and on time for all four quarters. (Although quarterly liabilities of $100 or less for the first three quarters may be carried over to the next quarter rather than deposited without affecting the right to the automatic extension.) To get the extension, an employer whose fourth quarter liability is $100 or less must deposit the amount owed by January 31 rather than send in payment with Form 940.

For good cause, the IRS will grant extensions of up to 90 days, so long as an application for the extension was filed by the due date of the form. Regardless of the filing extension, however, all FUTA tax payments must be made on time.

Where must Form 940 be filed?

Form 940 should be mailed, sent by private delivery service, or hand delivered to the IRS Service Center for the region where the employer has its principal place of business.

How to amend incorrect Forms 940.

Employers that make an error on Form 940 and need to file an amended return can do so by filing a new Form 940 for the same year as the year being amended with the correct numbers. Check the box above Part I indicating an amended return is being filed, and attach a statement explaining why the amended return is necessary.

If claiming a refund of overpaid taxes, the employer must attach Form 843, Claim for Refund and Request for Abatement.

Employers that go out of business.

Employers that cease doing business must file a Form 940 for the portion of the last calendar year they were in business and check the box on the line below Question C above Part I indicating no future returns will have to be filed. A statement needs to be attached specifying the following:

>» The location where required records will be kept;

>» Who is responsible for keeping the records; and

>» The name and address of the purchaser of the business or the fact that there was no purchaser or that the purchaser's name is unknown.

Form 940 Line-by-Line Instructions

In addition to Questions A through C which determine whether the employer can file Form 940-EZ, Form 940 contains:

>» Part I—Computation of Taxable Wages;

>» Part II—Tax Due or Refund;

>» Part III—Record of Quarterly Federal Unemployment Tax Liability; and

>» Form 940V—Payment Voucher.

Part I is used to list total payments less exempt payments and payments over $7,000 to determine the total taxable wages.

Part II is used to calculate the employer's total FUTA tax as well as any balance due or overpayment. The employer must calculate the gross FUTA tax and determine what credits are available to reduce the tax liability. Line 3 of Part II consists of columns that require information regarding state unemployment taxes paid during the year. This information is needed to properly calculate the appropriate credit available to the employer.

Part III is completed only if the employer's total FUTA tax (gross tax less credits) is over $100.

Form 940-V is to be completed only if you are sending any payment with the completed Form 940 (fourth quarter liability of $100 or less). Checks should be made out to the "United States Treasury".

Penalties for FUTA Noncompliance

In addition to paying the FUTA tax actually owed to the IRS, there are several penalties associated with late deposits, payments, and filing of returns.

Late filing of Form 940

Unless there is reasonable cause and no willful neglect, late filing of Form 940 or 940-EZ results in an "addition to tax", the amount of which depends on how late the return is filed.

»The amount is 5% of the amount of tax required to be shown on the return (reduced by any timely deposits and credits) for each month or fraction of a month the return is late, up to a maximum of 25%.

»Fines increase to 15% per month up to a maximum of 75% if the late filing is fraudulent.

Failure to pay FUTA tax

Unless there is reasonable cause and no willful neglect, late payment of tax owed as shown on the Form 940 or 940-EZ results in an "addition to tax", the amount of which depends on how late the payment is made.

»0.5% of any unpaid tax shown on the return (after accounting for credits) for each month or fraction of a month the payment is late, up to a maximum of 25%.

»An additional 0.5% per month of any unpaid tax not shown on the return but for which the IRS has issued a notice and demand, if the tax is not paid within 21 calendar days of the notice and demand (10 business days if the amount is at least $100,000), up to a maximum of 25%.

»These additions to tax for failure to pay taxes are doubled to 1% per month or fraction of month for amounts remaining unpaid after 10 days after the employer receives a notice of intent to levy from the IRS or 1 day after the day the employer receives a notice and demand for immediate payment from the IRS.

Failure to file and pay

In any month where an employer is subject to additions to tax both for failure to file Form 940 and a failure to pay FUTA tax, the addition for failure to file is reduced by 0.5% of the unpaid tax.

Reasonable cause

To avoid additional taxes for late filings or tax payments the employer must make an affirmative statement under penalty of perjury setting forth all the facts supporting the claim of reasonable cause for its failure. Facts must show the employer "exercised ordinary business care and prudence".

Accuracy-related penalty

Employers can also be assessed an accuracy-related penalty of 20% of the understated amount that can be attributed to the employer's negligence or disregard of rules or regulations. This penalty can be imposed in addition to a penalty for filing a late return, but not in addition to a fraud penalty.

Failure to make timely FUTA deposits

Unless there is reasonable cause and no willful neglect, late deposits of

FUTA tax are subject to a penalty in addition to the tax owed that depends on the lateness of the deposit.

>> 2% of the undeposited amount if it is paid within 5 days of the due date;

>> 5% of the undeposited amount if it is paid within 6-15 days of the due date;

>> 10% of the undeposited amount if it is paid more than 15 days after the due date; or

>> 15% of the undeposited amount if it is not paid within 10 days after the employer receives its first IRS delinquency notice or on the same day a notice for demand for immediate payment is received.

>> The 10% penalty for depositing FUTA tax more than 15 days after the due date also applies to employers who are mandated to make federal tax deposits electronically but use a paper check and deposit coupon instead, even if the paper deposit is made timely.

Relief for certain small, new depositors.

The IRS may waive the failure-to-deposit penalty for an employer's inadvertent failure to make a deposit of FUTA taxes for certain small, new depositors. The failure-to-deposit penalty may also be abated for an employer of any size that sends its first payroll tax deposit to the IRS rather than depositing it with the appropriate government depository.

State Unemployment Insurance (SUI or SUTA)

Although the Federal Unemployment Tax Act provides a framework for state funding and coverage requirements, states each have their own methods for determining tax rates, wage bases, and benefit eligibility and amounts.

The Employment Relationship

Employers within a state are generally covered by the state's unemployment insurance program if they meet the requirements for coverage under FUTA, although some states provide even broader terms for coverage. But even if an employer is subject to a state's unemployment insurance law, it is covered only to the extent its workers are performing covered services as employees rather than independent contractors.

Employees Working In More Than One State

There are four factors employers can use in determining to which state an employee should be "allocated" for unemployment insurance purposes:

»*Are services "localized"?* An employee's services are localized within a state if services performed outside the state are merely incidental to services performed within the state. If services are localized, the employer is subject to the unemployment insurance law of that state for the employee and other allocation factors need not be considered.

»*Does the employee have a "base of operations"?* If the employee has a single base of operations in a state where he or she works, that state's unemployment insurance law governs. A base of operations can be the place where an employee reports to work or returns from work, or a place where the employee has an office, receives instructions from the employer, receives mail and supplies, or keeps business records.

»*Is there a "place of direction or control"?* If the employee's work is not localized and there's no base of operations, the next factor to analyze is whether there is a place of direction or control in one of the states where the employee performs services.

»*What is the employee's "state of residence"?* In those rare instances where none of the three previous factors can be applied, the state of the employee's residence has jurisdiction if the employee performs some work there.

Reciprocal coverage arrangements

In some instances there are reciprocal coverage arrangements that allow employers to choose the state of coverage for certain multistate workers who move from state to state.

SUI Taxable Wages

FUTA requires that each state's taxable wage base must at least equal the FUTA taxable wage base of $7,000 per employee, and most states have wage bases that exceed the required amount.

Contribution Rates and Experience Rating

The contribution rate is the rate an employer applies to its taxable payroll to determine the amount of unemployment taxes it must pay. The rate is determined by the employer's "experience rating", which is based on the employer's unemployment benefit charges and average annual taxable payroll. The experience rating system is based on the insurance principle that premiums (contribution rates) are based on the risk involved (unemployment benefits charged to the employer).

The states use one of four methods to determine an employer's experience rate:

Reserve ratio.

The majority of states use this method. Each employer is assigned an account, into which it pays unemployment taxes. The account is then reduced by unemployment benefits paid to the employer's former employees during the year. The reserve ratio is the balance (reserve) in the employer's account divided by the employer's average taxable payroll for a specific period of years (usually three), expressed as a percentage.

$$\text{Reserve ratio} = \frac{\text{Unemployment taxes paid—Benefits charged}}{\text{Average taxable payroll}}$$

The ratio determines the employer's unemployment tax rate according to tables issued by the state. The higher the ratio, the lower the tax rate.

Benefit ratio method

The next most popular experience rating method, this method considers the relationship between the unemployment benefits charged to the employer during a stated period and the employer's total taxable payroll for the same period (taxes paid are not part of the equation).

$$\text{Benefit ratio} = \frac{\text{Benefits charged}}{\text{Total taxable payroll}}$$

The lower the benefit ratio, the lower the tax rate as determined by referencing tax rate tables issued by the state.

Benefit wage ratio method

This method is only used by two states and focuses on the taxable wages used to determine the benefits payable to employees, rather than the benefits themselves. These wages are then compared to the employer's total taxable payroll during the same period.

$$\text{Benefit wage ratio} = \frac{\text{Benefit wages paid}}{\text{Total taxable payroll}}$$

The lower the benefit wage ratio, the lower the tax rate.

Payroll stabilization

Alaska is the only state that uses this method. Under this method, an employer's tax rate is determined by fluctuations in its payroll from quarter to quarter and year to year. As payroll decreases the tax rate increases. If the payroll remains stable or increases, the tax rate will not increase and may decrease.

Voluntary Contributions

Employers in 26 states can make voluntary contributions to their unemployment tax accounts. These contributions increase the balance in those accounts, which in turn improve the employer's reserve ratio and decrease their unemployment tax rates. The goal is to change the employer's bracket on the state's unemployment tax rate table, which corresponds to the next lower tax bracket.

Joint or Combined Accounts

For employers having more than one affiliated subsidiary in a state, an attractive option for reducing unemployment contributions may be to join the subsidiaries for unemployment insurance purposes. Not all states offer the joint account option.

The Unemployment Benefits Process

Eligibility for benefits

Requirements for claimants for unemployment benefits to become and remain eligible for benefits include:

> »Earning a certain amount of wages in the "base period";

> »Being involuntarily unemployed for reasons other than misconduct connected with their work;

> »Filing a claim for benefits;

> »Registering for work with the state unemployment security office;

> »Being physically and mentally able to work;

> »Be looking for and available for work (other than during times of job training or jury duty);

> »Not being unemployed because of a labor dispute other than a lockout; and

> »Being truthful in applying for benefits

The Department of Labor allows states to pay unemployment compensation to parents who take time off from work to be with newborn or newly-adopted children.

Benefit amounts

Generally, benefits can be collected for 26 weeks, unless extended because the claimant has a part-time job or the federal government has granted an emergency extension during periods of high unemployment.

> »*Part-time employees get benefits.* Employees whose hours are reduced are eligible, as long as they are not earning more than the weekly benefit amount.

> »*Other payments can reduce benefits.* Certain payments provided by the employer can make the employee ineligible for unemployment benefits until the period covered by the payments has expired. Such payments

may include holiday pay, vacation pay, dismissal or severance pay, and payments in lieu of notice.

Benefit charges to employers

If the claimant's base period wages were all earned from one employer that employer's unemployment tax account is charged with all the benefits received by the former employee. In situations where the claimant has been employed by more than one employer during the base period, state uses several different methods to allocate benefit charges.

Auditing benefit charge accounts

Periodic statements issued by the state showing benefits charged against the employer's account should be audited thoroughly for errors, including:

» Individuals who get benefits and wages in the same week;

» A charge to the account even though a protest against the claim remains unresolved;

» Benefits received by a claimant during the disqualification period;

» Two charges to the account for the same benefits;

» Benefits paid beyond the maximum allowed by law; and

» Incorrect account number

Challenging benefit claims

Employers can reduce their unemployment tax costs by making sure they challenge benefit claims for which they believe the former employee is ineligible. When faced with a claim for unemployment benefits, the employer should:

» Be complete and truthful in listing the grounds for an employee's termination;

» Document any and all evidence of misconduct;

» Respond to notices and requests for information within the time frame allowed;

» Detail any final payments made to terminated employees; and

» Prod the unemployment agency to make sure the claimant is looking for work.

Reporting Requirements

Each state requires employers to submit quarterly contribution and wage reports containing some or all of the following information:

» Total wages paid;

» Taxable wages paid;

» Nontaxable wages paid;

» Number of employees each month;

» Gross wages for each employee;

» Taxable/nontaxable wages breakdown for each employee; and

» Number of weeks worked by each employee.

Multiple worksite reporting

Employers with more than one worksite must also file quarterly employment and wage reports with the state employment security agency that break down the information by industry and locality. The federal Bureau of Labor Statistics uses this information.

State Disability Insurance

Five states plus Puerto Rico provide benefits to employees who are temporarily disabled by a nonwork-related illness or injury through a tax-supported state fund.

CHAPTER 8

Compliance

Employer Identification Numbers

How to get an EIN

New employers that have not been assigned an EIN must apply for one by completing form SS-4, Application for employer Identification Number. It must be sent within seven days after the employer first pays wages, at the LATEST.

An employer can also

Obtain an EIN by calling the IRS's Tele-TIN program, which process application for EINs by telephone. This allows for immediate assignment, and use of an employer's EIN. The employer still MUST complete and send in the Form SS-4. *Only those individuals who can sign an employment tax return are authorized to receive an EIN over the phone.*

When there is no EIN

If an employer has not received its EIN before the due date of a deposit return, the employer should write "applied for" in the space provided for the EIN and also note the date of the application.

IRS waives signature requirement for form SS-4

The IRS has temporarily waived the signature requirement in hopes of developing other methods of filing for an EIN. Eventually the IRS will provide procedures for accepting signatures in digital or other electronic form.

Use ONE EIN

Regardless of the number of businesses the employer is operating or trade names it is using, only one Form SS-4 and one EIN is used. However, this general rule does not apply to separate but affiliated corporations, which each need an EIN.

Mergers, consolidations, and reorganizations

The proper EIN to use after a corporate merger or acquisition depends on its characterization under the IRC. If the merger is a reorganization under the IRC, the surviving corporation should use its previously assigned EIN. However, a new EIN is necessary if a new corporation emerges from a consolidation that does not qualify as reorganization.

Depositing Withheld Income and Employment Taxes

The payment of withheld federal income, social security, and Medicare taxes, as well as the employer's share of social security and Medicare taxes and FUTA tax, is handled differently from the payment of other federal taxes. Rather than paying the taxes when filing a return, employers generally must deposit the taxes in a federal depository, unless the amounts are very small (eg. FUTA tax liability less than $100 which can be paid with the 940 tax return)

Payroll Tax Deposit Rules

Monthly or semiweekly depositor status: Employers are assigned a depositor status classification. The determination is based on the employer's total liability for federal income, social security and Medicare taxes during the "look back period" and generally lasts for an entire calendar year. The look back period is the 12-month period running from July 1 of the second previous year through June 30 of the previous year.

Adjustments found on a Form 941 through Form 941X corrections are applied only to the look back period during which the Form 941X was filed, not to the quarter, which the Form 941 is correcting. Therefore, adjustments to the last quarter of the look back period made in the next look back period are not considered as part of the initial look back period when determining an employer's deposit status.

Non-payroll withholding treated separately. In addition to withholding from wages, employers also must withhold federal income tax from several types of "non-payroll" payments it makes (backup withholding, gambling winnings, pensions, annuities, IRAs, and other deferred income, etc). Withholding on these items is not reported on the 941, but annually on the Form 945.

New employers are classified as monthly depositors because they have no tax liability experience during the look back period.

A successor with the same EIN as its predecessor company has the same deposit requirements as the predecessor.

A successor with a new EIN is a new employer and should deposit as a monthly depositor until the status changes.

Different look back period for railroad & farm employers

Monthly depositors must deposit their accumulated tax liability for each calendar month by the 15th of the following month. *(more than $50,000 in liability during the look back period)*

Semiweekly depositors *(more than $50,000 in liability during the look back period)* must deposit employment taxes for wages paid on Wednesday, Thursday, and Friday by the following Wednesday. If paid on Saturday, Sunday, Monday and Tuesday must be deposited by the following Friday.

One-day deposit rule applies when employer's tax liability reaches $100,000 on any day during a monthly or semiweekly deposit period, the taxes MUST be deposited by the close of the next banking day. If a monthly depositor, then employer becomes semi-weekly depositor for the remainder of the year.

Semiweekly periods bridging two quarters: this happens when a pay period from one quarter overlaps into another quarter. If employer has 2 paydays, then employer would have 2 tax deposits. (does anyone really do that?)

Quarterly "de minimus" deposit rules: Employers with an accumulated tax liability of less than $2,500 for any quarter can deposit the liability according to their monthly or semiweekly depositor status or pay it with their form 941 return.

Saturday, Sunday, and Holiday extension. The deposit is due the next banking day.

Shortfall rule

The IRS allows a "safe harbor" shortfall so employers are not penalized for depositing a small amount less than the entire amount of their deposit obligation. An employer satisfies its deposit obligation if the amount of the shortfall is no more than the greater of $100 or 2% of the entire amount due, so long as the original deposit is made timely and the shortfall is deposited by the appropriate "make-up date." For semiweekly depositors, the shortfall must be deposited by the first Wednesday or Friday occurring on or after the 15th of the month after the month during which the original deposit was required to be made or, if earlier, by the due date of the quarterly employment tax return (e.g. Form 941). Semiweekly depositors cannot send in the shortfall payment with their 941, it must be deposited.

Determining the timeliness of deposits. Considered timely if received by an authorized financial institution before the due date.

How to Deposit Payroll Taxes

The federal reserve no longer accepts federal tax deposits

Must be paid to a financial institution authorized to accept federal tax deposits.

The vast majority of employers pay electronically through EFTPS *(replacing FTD coupons)*, once triggered; EFT is a MUST for all depository taxes. The Treasury Agents are Bank of America and BankOne.

>> Enrolling in EFTPS is done by completing Form 9779, a separate form for each EIN number and a separate form for each tax type. When processed the TFA *(Treasury Financial Agent)* will send the employer Form 9787 Confirmation/update form.

>> EFTPS Payment options - ACH Debit or ACH Credit

  – ACH Debit—Employer gives TFA information to take money from their account

  – ACH Credit—Employer instructs Financial Institution to send money to TFA. Once an employer timely and accurately requests an ACH Credit entry, the financial institution is responsible for the timely origination of the ACH credit entry with the appropriate account number and the correct format.

>> Electronic Tax Application—if something goes wrong and you want your payment to be made timely, you could try ETA. ETA is a subsystem of EFTPS that receives, processes, and transmits federal tax deposits and related information for employers that make same day deposits through Fedwire value transfers, Fedwire non-value transactions, and Direct Access transactions. Deemed to be made on the date the payment is received by the Federal Reserve Bank

>> ***No More Mag Tape Deposits!!!***

>> Paper Deposits—Use Form 8109 Coupon

Smaller employers *(less than $200,000 in payroll)* and new businesses can continue to use paper checks and deposit coupons

Making deposit before EIN is assigned

Must make the deposits with the IRS service center where they will file their returns, rather than a financial institution. Must be accompanied by an explanation, with check or money order made payable to the US Treasury, showing the employer name, address, kind of tax, calendar quarter covered, and the date the EIN was applied for. Use Form 8109-B

Depositing non-payroll withheld taxes

Treat different than payroll taxes, each type of tax creates a separate deposit obligation and a separate FTD coupon is needed. Forms 8109 and 8109-B include a separate box in the "type of Tax" section labeled "945" for non-payroll withheld taxes. Also use 8109-B when preprinted coupons are not available.

Federal Holiday procedures

If due date falls on holiday, the employer must initiate payment one business day before the holiday so that it will be effective on the first business day after the holiday.

Instrument of payment

Cash, postal money order, check drawn on and payable to the depository. (a check drawn on another bank can only be used if the depository will accept it for immediate payment) personal checks are not considered made until the check clears and funds are available. Federal Reserve banks no longer accept federal tax deposits.

Proof of payment
»ACH debit or ACH credit

–Financial Institution provide a statement to the employer or you can use a copy of the transfer showing a decrease in the employer's account balance, a record of the amount and date of the transfer and the US Government as the payee.

»For ETA payment

–A statement from the FRB that executed the transfer that shows the amount, date and identifies the US Government as the payee.

Refunds and reversals
»EFTPS - no refunds of overpayment will be made through EFTPS. Employers should make refund requests using current tax refund procedures (Form 843 and 941X)

»ACH Debit or ACH Credit—governed by the ACH rules. Employer has up to 5 banking days to reverse that payment if an error has been made, such as duplication of payment, wrong entity, or incorrect dollar amount. However, the reversal cancels the entire payment and if a new payment for the correct amount is not made timely, the employer will face a late deposit penalty. The IRS encourages employers to use the current paper method for requesting a refund in the event of an overpayment.

Recordkeeping diligence a must

Keep meticulous records of the instructions they give to financial institutions and TFAs to initiate EFTPS tax deposits.

Depositing FUTA taxes

Same manner as withheld income, social security and Medicare taxes although the due dates are different. Must be accompanied by the FTD coupon.

Penalties for Failure to Deposit on Time

» 2% of undeposited amount if deposited within 5 days of due date

» 5% of undeposited amount if deposited within 6-15 days of due date

» 10% of undeposited amount if deposited more than 15 days after due date

» 15% of undeposited amount if it is not paid within 10 days after the employer received its first IRS delinquency notice.

100% penalty for not withholding and paying taxes. Known as the "Trust Fund Recovery Penalty" or the "100% penalty" for the "responsible person". IRS definition of "responsible person" takes into consideration the individual duties and authority. It excludes non-owners who work under the direction of a manager, although they may have check signing authority, and other employees who merely perform clerical task related to payroll and finance. For the 100% penalty to apply, the "responsible person" must have acted willfully in not withholding and paying over trust fund taxes. But willfulness does not necessarily mean an intent to defraud the government. Paying other creditors rather than depositing taxes is a willful failure to pay, even though the payments are made to keep the business from failing. Also, reasonable cause is not a defense to an assessment of the 100% penalty.

» Notice must be given before penalty is assessed. The 100% penalty notice must notify the "reasonable person" in writing, by mail, or in person at least 60 days before issuing a notice and demand for such penalty

» Liability for penalty may be shared. If IRS determines that a "reasonable person" is liable for the 100% penalty, it must disclose to that person (if a written request is made) the following information regarding the same failure to withhold and pay over payroll taxes:

– The names of other responsible persons

– Whether the IRS has attempted to collect the penalty from these other persons

−How much has been collected

»There is relief for volunteer board members directors.

»Criminal penalty—in addition to the 100% penalty, responsible persons who willfully fail to collect and pay over taxes are guilty of felony and can be fined up to $10,000 and/or imprisoned for up to 5 years.

If an employer is required to deposit employment taxes electronically uses a check and a paper deposit coupon instead, the employer is subject to the 10% failure to deposit penalty because failed to make the deposit in the correct manner, even if paper deposit was made on time.

Employer cannot shift deposit liability to payroll service provider. It does not matter that the employers delegated their employment tax responsibilities to an agent, the employer is still responsible. The IRS also states any refunds of penalties due would be paid to the employer and not the service provider.

Relief for certain small new depositors—IRS may waive penalty if:

»Net worth is less than $7 million *(or $2 million if employer is individual)*

»Failure to deposit occurs during the first quarter the employer is required to deposit, or the first deposit after a frequency change

»The return of the tax is filed by the due date

»Proof of reasonable cause—statement must be filed with IRS District director or the director of employer's IRS service center, who will make a determination whether there was reasonable cause for the failure to deposit

Applying current deposits to earlier under-deposits—The IRS automatically applies deposits to satisfy any under deposits from earlier quarters, including safe-harbor shortfalls (the oldest first), before applying it to the current obligation. The IRS then determines whether a late deposit penalty should be assessed. This means if employer is depositing current tax obligations in full, the employer may still be liable for a late deposit penalty for the portion that was applied to a previous obligation. Once an employer receives a penalty notice from IRS, it has 90 days to designate how its deposits are applied.

Applying overpayments from previous quarters—generally overpayments are also credited to past due under-deposits during the same quarter. If at the end of the quarter, the last deposit for the quarter results in an over-deposit for the quarter, it becomes an overpayment and a credit will be issued when the return is filed or the IRS will apply the overpayment to earlier under deposits in succeeding quarters if the employer elects on the 941 to have the overpayment applied to that quarter rather than to receive a refund.

The Employer's Employment Tax Return—Form 941

The purpose of Form 941 is to provide the IRS with a report of each employer's total taxable wages paid and payroll tax liability, which can be matched against the employer's record of tax deposits and wage and tax information provided to employees on their W-2 forms.

Exxemptions to Who Must File Form 941

»Seasonal employers *(must check seasonal employer box above line 1)*

»Businesses that withhold federal income tax
    from non-payroll items (backup withholding,
    pensions, annuities, gambling winnings)

»Employers that report withheld taxes on domestic workers

»Employers that report wages from employee in US territories and
    possessions outside the continental US, plus Puerto Rico

»Agricultural employers, unless they also have
    employees who are not agricultural employees

»New Employers—write "applied for" and the date of
    application in the space provided for the EIN.

Merger/Acquisitions

If an employer sells or transfers its business, a separate form 941 must be filed; by BOTH the previous and current owners for the quarter during which the sale took place. Each employer must report only the wages it paid and taxes it withheld. The previous employer must attach a statement providing the new owner's name, the form of new business, the type of change that took place, and the date of the change.

When two companies merge or consolidate, the firm that results must file the 941 for the quarter during which the change took place, reporting the wages paid and taxes withheld by both companies. And submit a statement providing the type of change that took place, and the date of the change, and the absorbed company's name, address and EIN.

Acquisitions where successor hires predecessor's employees; under standard procedure, the successor and predecessor will each file a 941 for the quarter of the acquisition, reporting only the wages paid and taxes withheld by each.

Employers going out of business should check box above line 1 when completing its last 941 indicating it will not file any returns in the future and enter the last date on which wages were paid. A statement showing the address where the employer's records will be kept, the name of the person keeping the records, and, if the business has been sold or transferred, the name and address of the new owner and the date of sale or transfer.

Who can sign a 941?

The individual owning the business *(Sole proprietorship)*

The president, vice president, other principle corporate officer *(Corporation)*.

Authorized member/partner of an unincorporated association or partnership having knowledge of the organization's affair.

A fiduciary if the employer is a trust or estate.

Agents can file on behalf of employer once authorization is granted. Employer must designate the agent on form 2678. *(appointment of Agent)*

Attorney, accountants, other representative, or employee not listed above must obtain proper power of attorney before completing 941 by using Form 2848, Power of attorney and declaration of representative.

Form 941 is no longer scanned but the IRS still encourages employers to use the preprinted forms.

Negative amounts should be put in parentheses.

Payments made with 941 can be made if an employer's total tax liability for a quarter is less than $2,500.

Monthly depositors may pay any lawful deposit shortfalls for the quarter with the 941 even if the amount exceeds $2,500.

Payments should be made by including Form 941-V, payment voucher with the following information:

> »EIN, or "applied for" and date
>
> »First four characters (letters or numbers) of the employer's business name
>
> »Darken the oval for the quarter for which the tax payment is made (only one)
>
> »Employer's name and address
>
> »Amount paid

Paying tax due with the 941, an employer cannot take advantage of the 10 day filing extension granted to employers that have deposited their entire tax liability on time throughout the quarter

When and Where to file the 941

In general the 941 must be filed by the last day of the first month following the end of each calendar quarter. However, if the employer has made timely deposits of all its payroll tax liability for the quarter, an automatic extension of the filing period to the 10th day of the next month is granted. The IRS will not grant any further extension.

If the 941 due date falls on a Saturday, Sunday, or legal holiday, the due date becomes the next business day. *(Same for the 10 day extension)*

The 941 is considered filed on the date of the postmark put on the envelope by the US Postal Service *(as long as it has full postage paid)*.

Private Deliver Services (PDS); are required to either record electronically to its data base the date on which an item was accepted for delivery or mark on the cover of the item the date on which it was given to the PDS for delivery. The date that is recorded or marked is treated as the postmark date for the "timely mailing, timely filing" rule; the current list includes:

> »Airborne Express—overnight air express, next afternoon service and second day service

> »DHL Worldwide Express—DHL "same day" service, and USA overnight

> »Federal Express—Fedex Priority Overnite, FedEx Standard Overnight, and Fedex 2nd day

> »United Parcel Service—UPS Next day air, UPS Next Day Air Saver, UPS 2nd day air, and UPS 2nd day air a.m.

Schedule B

Semiweekly depositors at any time during a quarter must file an attachment to the 941, the schedule B (employer's record of Federal Tax Liability). This includes monthly depositors that accumulate at least $100,000 in employment tax liability during a month.

The Schedule B records payroll tax liability, not deposits made.

Avoiding 941 Errors

Report separately the taxable social security wages and the social security tax on Lines 6a and 6b, the taxable social security tips and tax on lines 6c and 6d, and the taxable Medicare wages and tips and the Medicare tax on Lines 7a and 7b.

Use the most recent preprinted form 941, if done by a third-party preparer, make sure the name is printed exactly as it appears on the preprinted form.

Verify that line 13 is the sum of lines 5 and 10 minus line 12.

Verify the calculation of the social security tax on line 6b (12.4% (6.2% for each the employer and employee) multiplied by the social security wages) and the Medicare tax on Line 7b (2.9% (1.45% for each the employee and employer) multiplied by the Medicare wages and tips.

Never submit a form with an entry on both lines 15 and 16; employer cannot have balance due and a refund at the same time.

Always check totals on 941 against W3 or 6559 to make sure they match

Always sign the return and print the signing employee's name and title

Annual Reporting of Non-payroll Withholding (Form 945)

Non-payroll items have been removed from the 941 and are reported on the 945. *(pensions, annuities, gambling winnings, etc as well as backup withholding)*. Total deposits of these non payroll withheld taxes will also be reported on the 945, and any amount withheld that has not yet been deposited when the form is completed must be paid with the form.

The last section of the 945 is a monthly summary of tax liability.

Deposit status may be different from the 941.

945 are due by January 31st with an extension to February 10th for employers that have timely deposited all their non payroll withheld taxes for the year.

Monthly Reporting for Delinquent Employers—Form 941-M

Employers that fail to withhold or deposit taxes or file returns on time may be required by the IRS to report employment taxes monthly rather than quarterly, using the 941-M. The IRS will notify an employer of its monthly reporting requirement by sending form 2481 *(notice to make special deposit of taxes)*.

If required to report using the 941-M, all deposits must be made no more than 2 banking days after the payment of wages and must be made into a special deposit account providing a trust fund for the US Government.

Employers Operating Outside the Continental US—Forms 941-PR and 941-SS

Employers that have employees in Puerto Rico must file 941-PR.

Employers that have employees in American Samoa, Guam, Northern Mariana Islands, and the Virgin Islands must file form 941-SS.

Employers of Domestic Employees

Individuals who hire domestic employees must report and pay both the employer and employee share of social security and Medicare taxes on wages it pays these employees on their personal tax return, form 1040, Schedule H

Sole proprietors who file 941 for business employees may report the wages of their household employees as well

Annual Reporting by Agricultural Employers—Form 943

The 943 serves the same purpose as the 941 but it is for Agricultural Employers.

The 943 is filed annually rather than quarterly.

Employers with both agricultural and Non-Agricultural must file both the 941 and the 943.

943-A is completed in the same way as the Schedule B of Form 941, requiring an entry for each day payroll tax liability incurred during the year, as well as monthly and yearly totals.

Form 943 must be filed by the last day of the first month after the year being reported on the form *(Jan 31st)*.

Employers that have deposited all their taxes on time are entitled to an automatic 10 day extension.

The look back period for agricultural employers is the second calendar year proceeding the current calendar year *(may have two separate deposit requirements if they pay wages to both agricultural and non agricultural employees.)*

Making corrections to a 941 using 941X

FIT, SS, or Medicare discovered BEFORE the 941 is filed, must report and pay the proper withholding amount with the 941.

SS or Medicare tax under collected or underpaid discovered AFTER form 941 is filed, the adjustment is made by reporting the underpayment on the employer's timely filed form 941 for the quarter during which the error is discovered and paying the underpayment to the IRS at that time even if the money is never collected from the employee.

FIT under withheld discovered AFTER form 941 is filed, the employer can avoid paying interest on the under collection if it reports the under collection as an adjustment on its timely filed 941 for the quarter during which the error is detected. If not reported on the 941 for the quarter when the error is discovered, it should be reported on the next 941 with interest accruing from the due date of the earlier 941. In any event, it must be reported by the due date of the 941 for the 4th quarter of the year during which the error occurred.

Under withheld income tax must be withheld during the same calendar year the error occurred.

FIT, SS, Medicare tax over collected discovered before the 941 is filed, it does not have to report the over withheld amount if it repays the over withheld amount by the due date of the 941 and keeps in its records a receipt from the employee showing the date and amount of payment. The repayment must occur before the end of the calendar year during which the error was made.

Therefore, over withholding during the fourth quarter of the year must be discovered and repaid by 12/31 of the year, even though the 941 is not due until Jan 31st of the following year.

SS or Medicare tax over collected and discovered after 941 are filed, the employer must repay the over withheld amount or reimburse the employees by withholding less from the future wages. The repayment or reimbursement must be made by the end of the quarter following the quarter during which the over collection was discovered. If repayment is made in a year after the year the error was made, the employee will be issued a W-2-C.

FIT tax over collected and discovered after 941 is filed, the employer can either repay or reimburse the employee for the over with held amount, However, the employer must repay the over withheld amount before the end of the calendar year during which the error was made, as well as keep the employee's written statement as to the date and amount repaid. Employers that reimburse employees for over withheld amounts by reducing future withheld taxes can do so only during the same calendar year that the error occurred.

Making adjustments on 941; if an employer has properly repaid over withheld amounts to employees, it can claim a credit against taxes due y making an adjustment on Form 941 filed for the same calendar year the error occurred and was discovered. For SS or Medicare tax repayments, the adjustment must be made no later than the due date for the 941 filed for the quarter after the quarter during which the error was discovered.

Explaining the adjustments on 941X; the purpose of 941X is to explain the nature of the adjustment and show the erroneous and corrected amounts of tax withheld. If a written statement is attached instead of 941X it must include:

>»Circumstances of the error

>»Ending date of the quarter in which the error was made

>»The amount of error

>»The date error was discovered

>»How the FIT was handled

>»If SS or Medicare was repaid or the employee gave written consent to any refund or credit claimed by employer

>»If SS or Medicare occurred in an earlier year, a statement that the employee has state in writing that no claim of credit or refund has been or will be made regarding the over withholding

Employer refunds and credits, if the employer withholds the correct taxes, but mistakenly overpays the government, the employer can choose between a credit and a refund on the amount overpaid. This option is not available where the overpayment is due to the employer's over withholding of taxes. A credit for such a tax overpayment is taken as a deduction on the 941, which must be accompanied by a 941X explaining the reason for the credit. A refund of the tax overpayment is claimed on Form 843, which provides space for the employer to explain the reason for the refund.

If the credit or refund involves overpayment of the employee share of SS or Medicare tax, the employer must include a statement that the employee has consented in writing to the credit or refund or a statement that the tax has been repaid to the employee.

Penalties for Late reporting and Paying Tax

Late filing of employment tax returns

Unless the employer has reasonable cause and is not guilty of willful neglect, late filing of the 941 (or other employment tax) results in an "addition to tax", the amount of which depends on how late the return is filed.

Failure to pay employment taxes

Unless there is a reasonable cause and no willful neglect, late payment of tax owed as shown on an employment tax return results in and "addition to tax", the amount of which depends on how late the payment is made.In addition, if any portion of a tax under payment is due to the employer's negligence or disregard of IRS regulations, the employer will be assessed a penalty of 20% of the amount not paid that is attributable to the negligence or disregard. If any portion of the tax is not paid because of fraud, a penalty of 75% of the under payment due to fraud will be assessed. *(Both penalties cannot be assessed on the same underpayment) (But I bet they would try)*.

Failure to file and pay

In any month where an employer is subject to additions to tax both for a failure to file an employment tax return and a failure to pay tax, the addition for failure to file is reduced by .5% of the unpaid tax

Reasonable cause

An employer wishing to avoid the additional taxes for late filings or tax payments must make an affirmative statement under penalty of perjury setting forth all the facts supporting the claim of reasonable cause for its failure.

Interest

Any withheld FIT, SS, or Medicare that remains unpaid by the last date allowed for payment, accumulates interest from that date until the date paid at the federal short-term rate plus 3%. Interest on additions to tax that are assessed for failure to file the 941 on time accumulates from the due date of the return to the date of payment of the addition to tax. If the IRS makes a notice and demand for payment of the addition to tax, and the employer makes the payment within 21 calendar days of the notice and demand, interest stops accumulating on the date the notice and demand for payment is made.

Criminal penalties
Certain actions can bring criminal fines and imprisonment.

Information Reporting for Employees—W-2

Employers must provide W-2s
The IRC requires a W-2 to be provided by an employer engaged in trade or business that pays compensation to an employee for work performed, even if the employee is not paid in cash. *(There is no minimum amount that triggers reporting)*.

A W-2 is also required if the employer withheld FIT from the employee or would have done so if the employee had claimed no more than one withholding allowance.

When there has been a merger or consolidation of two employers and one survives, the survivor is considered to be the same employer as the absorbed company. Therefore, it must provide W-2 to all the employees who worked for the absorbed company and the survivor during the calendar year of the merger or consolidation, which contain the wages paid by both companies.

Where one company acquires another's business property and retains employees who worked for the acquired company, there are two options the companies can use in determining which is responsible for providing the W-2 forms to their employees and the government.

> »Standard procedure the predecessor makes a final payment of wages to its employees and reports the wages and tax withheld on a W-2. The successor reports only the wages and taxes it pays and withholds. W-4s used by the predecessor must be kept in its files for four years after the final wage payment, and new W-4s must be provided to the successor. The same retention rules apply to W-5s.

> »Alternative procedure is where the successor and predecessor can agree that, for employees continuing their employment with the successor, the successor will provide the W-2s that include wages paid and taxes withheld by both parties during the year of the acquisition. The predecessor must provide W-2 's only for the employees who do not work for the successor after the acquisition. Use of this procedure will mean both the predecessor and the successor will have different wage and tax amount totals for the 941s than for the W-2s. Each company should attaché a statement to its 941 explaining the reason for the different amounts, providing the name, address, and EIN of the other

company, referring to Revenue Procedure 96-60, which contains the standard and alternate procedures described.

–The predecessor must transfer to the successor all current W-4s that were provided to the predecessor by the employees who are working for the successor. The successor must use those forms to determine the proper amount of federal income tax withholding until the employee submits a revised form. If the W-4s were submitted to the predecessor during the quarter of the acquisition or the preceding quarter that must be provided to the IRS, the successor assumes that responsibility for the acquired employees.

Undeliverable W-2s—If an employer has been unable, after a reasonable effort to deliver the employee's W-2, it must keep those copies for four years. Mailing the W-2 to the employee's last known address is considered a reasonable effort to make delivery.

Reissued W-2s—If an employee loses the W-2 or it is destroyed, the employer can issue a new copy to the employee and should write, "Reissued Statement" on it. (Employers can charge employees for providing them with additional copies of a form that has been lost or destroyed).

Corrected W-2s—when an error is made on the W-2, the method of correction depends on when the correction is made.

» If Copy A of the form has not been sent to the SSA, the employer merely has to provide the employee with corrected copies with "corrected" written on them, check the "void" box on the original copy A, and send the new Copy A, with nothing extra written on it, to the SSA.

» If Copy A has already been filed with the SSA, the employer must use the W-2C to correct the error.

» Address Corrections—Do not need to correct with the SSA for just an address correction.

–Issue a new W-2, indicate "reissued Statement", DO NOT send copy A to SSA

–Issue a W-2C to employee with correct address. DO NOT send copy A to SSA

–Reissue W-2 with the correct address

When and Where to Furnish Form W-2

Copy A and Form W-3
Magnetic or electronic media containing Copy A is an information return

and must be sent to the Social Security Administration (not the employee or IRS). Due the last day in February or by March 31 if done electronically.

Copy B, C and 2
These are the employees copies and must be sent to the employee by January 31st.

> »Employees who terminate before year-end can wait till January 31st or request in writing, before the end of the year, the employer must send it within 30 days of the request.

Copy D
The employer retains for its own records.

Copy 1
Must be sent to the applicable state and/or local tax agencies, according to deadlines set forth by each state, along with a state annual return.

Employers going out of business face accelerated W-2 due dates—employers that cease paying wages face accelerated deadlines for providing W-2 to the SSA and their employees. Such employers are required to file their final form 941 by the end of the month following the end of the quarter during which they went out of business. They have to provide Copies B, C, and 2 to their employees by the same date. Copy A along with the transmittal document must be sent to the SSA by the end of the second month following the end of the quarter during which the employer went out of business.

Monthly filers that are required to file monthly tax returns on 941M must file their final return by the 15th of the calendar month following the end of the month during which they cease paying wags. Such employers must provide W-2s to their employees by the end of the month during which the final 941M is due. The employer must provide forms W-2 and either the W-3 or the 6559 to the SSA by the end of the second calendar month after the end of the month for which the final return is made.

When a successor employer acquires substantially all or a separate unit of a business and employs the predecessor's employees, the "standard procedure" for wage reporting are that each employer reports the wages it paid employees on the W-2. When this procedure is used, the predecessor employer is covered by the accelerated W-2 deadlines if it ceases paying wages. If the "alternate procedure" is used, whereby the successor assumes the W-2 filing responsibility for all the predecessor's employees that the successor continues to employ, and the predecessor ceases paying wages, the predecessor is covered by the accelerated W-2 deadlines, but only for the employees who are not hired by the successor. The successor is not covered by the accelerated deadlines unless it ceases paying wages later in the year. Where a final 941 is not filed because a merger does not involve the cessation of business operations but only a change in corporate or business form, the expedited filing requirements do not apply.

The expedited filing requirements do not apply to employers with respect to their domestic employees working in the employer's private home, or to their agricultural employees, since filing with respect to such employees are made on an annual basis.

If an employer has good cause to request an extension of the date for filing Copy A or magnetic media to the SSA, it should complete and file Form 8809 before the original due date. The IRS will respond in writing, either approving or denying an extension of up to 30 days. The employer can request a second 30-day extension by sending another 8809 during the first extension period and attaching a copy of the first approval letter.

Employers can also request an extension of the due date for providing W-2s to employees by sending a letter to the IRS on or before January 31st.

For employers that go out of business during the year and face an accelerated deadline for providing W-2s, and the employer is required to file its W-2s on magnetic media, the deadline for filing W-2s is extended to the later of the expedited date or October 31st, and the deadline for filing the W-2s to the SSA is extended to November 30th. These extensions do not apply to the furnishing of a W-2 to an employee who is requesting on in writing. These extensions are provided because the specifications for filing a W-2 on Magnetic media are generally unavailable until the 3rd quarter of the year.

When the due date falls on a weekend or holiday, the due date is extended until the next business day.

Miscellaneous Forms W-2 Issues

Hyphenation
When submitting paper W-2s to the SSA, the employer's EIN and the employee's SSN MUST include hyphens.

Dollar amounts
Should be entered without commas or dollar signs, but with decimals points and the cents portion must be shown. Always show cents, with .00 used for even dollar amounts. Beginning with 2001 W-2s, all money amounts will have the dollar signs printed on the form.

Magnetic media reporting
Employers filing 250 or more W-2s are required to file them on some form of magnetic media, either tape, diskette, or cartridge, or electronically.

Providing Wage and Tax Information to the SSA—Form W-3

Once an employer has provided its employees with their parts of the W-2, it must send Copy A of each form to the SSA. If filing paper, the employer must also send a W-3. All the W-2s and the W-3 constitute an information return. W-3 contains totals of the amounts reported on the Employer's W-2 forms, acting as a reconciliation of the W-2s.

The W-3 is NOT for Mag media filers. Only used for paper filers.

Where there has been a merger or consolidation during the year, only the surviving company should file a W-3, since it is also responsible for filing the W-2s for employees of the absorbed corporation.

When one employer has acquired another during the year, the successor and the predecessor should file a W3 only of the W-2s for which they are responsible.

Can use Substitute forms but they must comply with specifications similar to those of the Copy A of W-2.

When and Where to File the W-3
»The due date for filing W-3 is the last day in February. Therefore, the W3, along with Copy A of the W-2 must be sent together.

»Extensions may be granted by completing and sending the IRS form 8809; by the due date of the form.

»Form W3 may be filed by a payroll service bureau or paying agent on behalf of the employer.

Correcting Information Statements—W-2C and W3C
When Errors have been made on a previously filed W-2, the employer must correct them by filing a W-2C with an accompanied W-3C.

Even if the employer is submitting only one W-2-C, it must also send the Form W3C. But if the only correction being submitted is to employees' names and/or SSN, the W3-C should not be filed and the employees should be advised to correct the corresponding information on their original W-2.

If only changing an address the W-2-C does not have to be completed or filed.

If the data is only state or local data to be corrected, Copy A should not be sent to the SSA.

If an employee is given a new social security card following an adjustment to the employee's resident status that shows a different name or social security number, the employer needs to file a form W-2C for the most current year only. It is no longer necessary to file forms W-2-C for all prior years.

Magnetic media not required. Employers correcting 250 or more W-2s are not required to submit the W-2Cs on magnetic media or electronically.

Forms W-2C that cannot be delivered to employees after a reasonable effort to do so must be kept by the employer for four years

Box by box instructions for the W-2C are on Form

Blank boxes should be used to correct items such as advance earned income credit payments, deferred compensation (including nonqualified plan and 457 plan distributions), dependent care benefits, employee business expenses, benefits included in box 1, uncollected SS and/or Medicare taxes on tips, elective deferrals, sick pay not included as income, and the cost of GTL. Be sure to label each box with the name, number and code from the W-2 for each item being corrected.

W3-Cs must be sent with any W-2-C being sent to the SSA unless the only corrections are the employee's name and/or social security number. The purpose of the W3-c is to summarize the information on the individual W-2-c. If the only correction is to the employers EIN or a previously filed Form W3, it can be sent to the SSA by itself. If the EIN is the only info being corrected, the employer should complete only boxes A,B, D, E, and I, enter its phone number, and sign the form. A separate W3-c must be sent for each type of W-2 being corrected.

Decreases must be shown inside parentheses ( ). Zero amounts must be shown as –0– in any boxes being corrected. Explain the decrease in wages or taxable amounts in the box marked "explain decreases here" below the "local income tax box". If the corrections necessitate an adjustment on an employment tax return, check the "yes" box below the explanation and on the next line enter the date the return was filed. At the bottom of the form, there are boxes for the contact person, phone number, fax number, and email address.

The W3C may be filed by a payroll service bureau or paying agent on the employers behalf and sign the form for the employer.

Magnetic media is not required

The Reconciliation Process for Employers

To help prevent "out of balance" conditions and reduce their confrontations with the Federal and State agencies employers must periodically "reconcile" their wage and tax information. You should make sure the amounts withheld, deposited, paid and reported agree with each other. Performing reconciliation regularly throughout the year allows employers to correct discrepancies with time to spare before the process of preparing and filing quarterly and year-end tax and information returns begins, thus saving you from quarterly and year-end disasters.

With each pay period and tax deposit, the employer must ensure values produced by the automated payroll system agree with amounts taken from prior reconciliation and updated by amounts taken from the current payroll register and tax deposit ledger. Then, before the last tax deposit for each of the first three quarters of the year, the employer must determine whether its deposits for the quarter equal the tax liability that will be reported on the quarterly 941. If not, the difference should be added or subtracted from the last deposit of the quarter.

If an employer's totals from its four quarterly 941 do not agree with the totals from its W-2s for certain amounts, the IRS and/or the SSA will inquire as to why and expect corrections to be made. Example, Social Security and/or Medicare wages and/or tips, and Advance earned income credit.

Be careful because Line 2 of the 941 cannot be corrected or adjusted on subsequent 941s. [If a mistake was made on the original, since the only adjustments allowed are to FIT, SS, and Medicare taxes withheld.] This means that such mistakes will cause the Line 2 totals to disagree with the total wages reported on the W-2s. Although the IRS does not ask employers to reconcile these amounts, employer should document any errors to avoid confusing during the year-end processing.

It is a good idea to request an exception report showing any employees with negative wages or taxes at the Federal, State, or local level. Any negative amounts reported on a W-2 will cause the employee record to be dropped.

The 941s for the year, should agree with the W-2/W3 totals. The IRS provides the SSA with information it receives from the employers, including any 941Xs explaining adjustments made on the 941, and the SSA provides the IRS with W-2 data.

If discrepancies are found, letters are sent to the employer notifying it of the discrepancy and requesting a response. The SSA sends the notice if the employer's 941 totals are greater than those on the W-2/W3. The IRS sends the notice if opposite is true. The outcome is then forwarded to the IRS for action regarding possible penalties and other assessments. Employers that receive a reconciliation letter should review it and compare it with their records. If the employer finds an error, it should make the corrections instructed by the letter. Failure to respond may result in the assessment of additional taxes or the reduction of benefits payable to the employees when they retire or become disabled.

Audit of form 941 shows underreporting and erroneous refunds...be careful, computers are a wonderful thing, the IRS and SSA are comparing notes.

Information Returns for Non-employee Payments—1099 Series

Most reportable payments must be reported on a form in the 1099 series. Similar to W-2s, an annual 1099 information statement must be sent to the non-employee payee detailing the payments and any withholding, while a copy is sent to the IRS along with a transmittal (1096). The 1099 helps the IRS determine whether individuals are reporting all their taxable non-wage income on their personal income tax return.

Miscellaneous Payments Made by Businesses—Form 1099 Misc.

Service payments to individuals totaling at least $600 in a calendar year made to non-corporate entities for services to the business must be reported in Box 7 of the 1099 Misc. Non-employee compensation may be in the form of fees, commissions, or prizes and awards. Service payments made to corporations are NOT reportable, EXCEPT for payments to corporate health care providers and gross proceeds paid to incorporated law firms.

Payments to health care service suppliers or providers must be reported in Box 6 if they total $600 or more in a year, whether the payee is an individual or a corporation.

Royalty payments must be reported in Box 2 if they total at least $10 during the year.

Payments to attorneys or law firms that are not reportable as attorneys' fees in Box 7 or on the W-2 must be reported in box 14 of the 1099 Misc.

Prizes and awards of at least $600 must be reported in Box 3 if they are not given for services rendered, although certain charitable, scientific, artistic, and educational awards need not be reported if they are designated for transfer to a charitable organization or government subdivision. Also reported in Box 3 are other payments that do not meet the requirements of any other box, including payments made after an employee's death to the deceased employee's estate or beneficiary. Payments of at least $600 to jurors must also be reported in box 3.

Amounts withheld from non-employee compensation because the payee failed to provide a valid TIN, must be reported in box 4 of the 1099 Misc.

Copies B and 2 of the 1099 must be sent to the non-employee who received the payments by January 31st.

Copy A with a transmittal (1096) is filed with the IRS. A 1096 serves the same purpose as a W3 for employers with W-2s. It summarizes the information on the 1099s. A new form 1096 must be filed for each type of 1099 being filed.

Substitute forms can be used if they confirm to specifications set forth by the IRS.

Magnetic Media Reporting is required by employers with 250 or more 1099s, unless a waiver has been obtained.

Pension and Retirement Plan Distributions—1099-R

Payers who make distributions of retirement income must report those payment and any amount withheld for FIT on the 1099-R

Distributions from all types of retirement plans, as well as payments of matured annuity, endowment, and life insurance contracts, must be reported on the 1099-R.

Payers must report not only the entire amount distributed during the year, but also the separate taxable and non-taxable amounts distributed. The gross is entered in Box 1, the taxable amount in Box 2a, and the non-taxable amount in Box 5.

An amendment contained in the Small Business Job Protection Act of 1996 altered the reporting requirements for the 1099-R by stating that no form needs to be filed if the total distribution to the payee during the year is less than $10.

All employer contributions to a qualified retirement plan, as well as employee pre-tax contributions, plus the earnings on all plan contributions, are included in the taxable amount of a distribution. The non-taxable amount is the portion of the distribution attributable to employee after-tax contributions, which were already taxed as wages before the contribution was made.

There are two situations where the taxable and non-taxable amounts do not have to be reported separately.

»If the payor cannot, after a reasonable effort, determine the taxable amount, it should check box 2B and leave Box 2a and 5 blank unless the distribution is from a traditional IRA, SEP, or SIMPLE plan.

»If the first payment from the plan was made before January 1, 1993, the employer has the option of separating taxable and non-taxable distribution amounts.

Payors making a direct rollover of a plan distribution must report the amount distributed on Form 1099-R as it would any other distribution.

If the direct rollover distribution includes deductible voluntary employee contributions *(DECs)*, only one form 1099R is needed to report the direct rollover of the entire distribution. But if the DECs are actually distributed, they must be reported on a separate 1099R

Copies B, C, and 2 of the 1099R must be sent to the payee by January 31st.

Copy A with the 1096 transmittal is filed with the IRS.

A new form 1096 must be filed for each type of 1099 being filed.

Substitute forms are allowed if they conform to the specifications set forth by the IRS.

Magnetic Media reporting is required for employers filing 250 or more 1099 Rs.

Penalties for Incorrect or Late Information Returns and Statements

Because some copies of information statements and returns must be sent to the IRS or the SSA, while others are sent to the employees or other payees, there are distinct penalties imposed for failure to file in each situation. Failure to File Information Returns.

The severity of the penalty generally depends on how late the return is filed or how late the correct or complete information is provided to the IRS.

The lower maximum penalties apply to small businesses.

Where an employer "intentionally disregards" the information return filing requirements and willfully fails to file on time or to include the correct information, the penalty for each return is greater of $100 or 10% of the correct amount of tax required to be shown on the return.

There is no maximum penalty for willful violation.

In addition to facing penalties from the IRS, businesses that file fraudulent information returns can be sued by the payee named on the return for damages of at least $5,000 or the actual damages suffered by the payee, including costs of pursuing the action and attorneys' fees, if that is greater. The payee must file a copy of the complaint in the suit with the IRS at the same time it is filed with the court.

Employers are not penalized for timely filed returns with incorrect or incomplete information corrected before August 1st, up to the greater of 10 returns or .5% of the total number of information returns the employer must file during the year.

No penalty will be assessed against an employer for "inconsequential" errors or omissions on an information return. Errors are inconsequential when they do not prevent the IRS from processing the return or applying it to its intended use.

Penalties will be waived for an employer if it can prove there was a reasonable cause for the failure to file or to include complete or correct information on a return. The employer can prove reasonable cause by showing there were "mitigating factors" leading to the failure. Events beyond the employer's control.

Employers have 45 days to respond to a penalty notice. Interest does not accrue until an actual penalty is assessed, not while it is still a proposal. Employers receiving the notice must submit a written explanation to show why the proposed penalties should not be assessed. IF the IRS accepts the explanation, it will send the employer a letter explaining that no further action is necessary.

If the employer's explanation provides an acceptable reason for part of the proposed penalty, the assessment will be for the difference. If the explanation is not accepted, the IRS will assess the full amount of the penalty. The IRS will also assess the penalty if the employer does not reply to the notice.

Failure to Provide Information Statements to Employees

If an employer fails to provide an employee or other payee with a required information statement, on time and/or with correct or complete information, a penalty of $50 per statement may be imposed, up to a maximum of $100,000. Only one penalty is assessed per statement, even if both a "failure to furnish timely" and a "failure to include correct information" have occurred.

No lower maximums for Small Businesses

Willful failures bring higher penalties

No "de minimis" exception is allowed to correct errors on a small number of information statements without penalty

No penalty will be assessed against an employer for "inconsequential" errors or omissions of an information statement.

No penalty for errors due to reasonable cause

Fraud brings criminal and civil penalties

Magnetic Media Reporting Requirements

Employers that file 250 or more forms must file them on some form of magnetic media.

It is important to note that the 250-return threshold does not mean the employer must have 250 employees at the time W-2s are filed. An employer with fewer than 250 employees could have high turnover during the year and may well have to file at least 250 W-2s, if so, they are required to file them on magnetic media. Also, the 250-form threshold applies to each type of form separately, not in total.

There are exceptions based on hardship.

8 inch and 5 ¼ inch diskettes are no accepted to file W-2s

An employer may file for extension

There are no requirements for W-2cs to be filed on magnetic media even if there are more than 250 forms.

Requirements are extended to the US possessions

Employers that file Copy A of their W-2s on magnetic tapes or cartridges must send along with each magnetic media report a Form 6559 Transmitter Report. The 6559 serves the same purpose as the W3, summarizing the wage and tax information on the W-2s. If an employer submits more than on magnetic media file, it must complete and file a separate form 6559 for each file.

The SSA has offered employers guidance on avoiding corrections, additional cost, and penalties when submitting mag media reports for the W-2s.

If an employer fails to file returns on magnetic media despite being required to do so, the failure is considered a failure to file a return, even if paper form W-2s have been submitted timely. As with failures to file a return, the amount of the penalty per return depends on how long it takes the employer to correct the failure.

DO NOT SEND BOTH PAPER AND MAG MEDIA, the SSA will process both sets of information and serious complications will result for the employees and the employer.

SSA will correct minor errors or omissions in wage reports submitted on magnetic media without sending them back to the employer. The errors SSA will correct the EIN, type of employment, year, and establishment numbers. The SSA will use the information on the 6559 to make the corrections.

SSA is informing employers of up to 500 mismatches of name and social security number per submitted wage report. The SSA hopes to provide employers a complete list of mismatches in the future.

Employers have the option of filing the W-2s electronically, using a personal computer and a modem, through SSAs BSO (Online Wage Reporting Service). You must register first.

Employers filing 250 or more of a single type of 1099 must file them on magnetic media or by electronic transmission.

Large food or beverage establishments (10 or more employees), where tipping is customary must file a Form 8027 (annual info return of Tip Income and allocated tips), to determine if tips have been underreported and must be allocated. A separate form must be filed for each establishment owned by the restaurant, and if 20 or more must file, they must be filed magnetically or electronically.

While employers are not required to file their employment tax and non-payroll tax returns on magnetic tape, employer agents may do so on their behalf...must apply first.

Form 941 e-file program; reporting agents can electronically file 941s

>>Accepts current returns

>>Late returns for the current year

>>And returns for any quarter in the previous year

>>Does not accept amended returns, corrected
   returns, or schedule Bs

Must apply first

The due dates are the same as those under the paper 941. It is not considered filed until it has been acknowledged as accepted for processing by the IRS.

941s can be filed by telephone.

Reporting "Special Wage Payments" to the SSA

Special wage payments refer to payment made to an employee or former employee that the employee earned in a prior year.

Significant impact on a retired employee, unless the SSA is notified about such payments. The retiree's benefits can be reduced when the SSA applies the annual earnings test.

SS benefits are meant to replace, in part, earnings lost due to retirement. Therefore, the amount of benefits which a beneficiary under 65 may receive each year depends on the amount the beneficiary's earned income, with benefits being reduced when earned income exceeds a certain limit. However, wages or payments received in one year but earned in a previous year are not counted under the "annual earnings test".

The annual earnings limits are determined by the SSA for age 62 *(full retirement)* and for retirees in the year they reach full retirement age, there is no earnings limit.

Examples of "special wage payments" are bonuses, accumulated vacation or sick pay, severance pay, back pay, standby pay, sales commissions, stock options, payments on account of retirement, or deferred comp reported on W-2 for one year but earned in a prior year.

Guidance for reporting special wages can be found in IRS pub 957.

Employers must report special wage payment for FIT, SS, and Medicare in the year the payments are received, on W-2.

The employer must report to SSA special wage payment made during the year to retired employees and employees still working while collecting social security benefits.

May be reported on magnetic computer tape or 3480 cartridges *(not diskettes)*

A paper listing can be used

Employers can use Form SSA-131 to report special wage payments to one employee. The form should be used to report nonqualified deferred comp and 457 plan deferrals and payments that could not be reported in box 11 of the W-2, but only if the employee also received special wage payments during the tax year.

CHAPTER 9

Deductions

Involuntary Deductions

Involuntary deductions are those over which an employer or employee has no control. The employer is required by law to deduct a certain amount of the employee's pay and send (remit) it to a person or government agency to satisfy the employee's debt.

Tax Levies

Employees who fail to timely pay their taxes may become subject to a federal or state tax "levy". The levy requires their employer to deduct the amount owed *(plus penalties and interest)* from their wages and remit it to the proper government agency. The employer must determine:

> »The amount of the employee's wages that is subject to the levy; and

> »Whether there are other claims on the employee's wages that take priority over the levy.

Federal tax levies. A federal tax levy is accomplished by "garnishing" or "attaching" an employee's wages to the extent that they are not exempt from levy. The employee's employer receives notice of the levy when the IRS sends Form 668-W, *Notice of Levy on Wages, Salary, and Other Income.*

Form 668-W consists of six parts.

> »Part 1 is the employer's copy, informing the employer of the amount of the levy and the employer's obligation to withhold and remit the levy amount.

> »Parts 2-5 must be given to the employee.

> –Part 2 is the employee's copy of the levy notice

–Parts 3-5 require the employee to provide information to the employer and the IRS regarding his or her tax filing status and any dependents who can be claimed as personal exemptions *(except children covered by a child support order against the employee that takes priority over the levy).*

–Parts 3 and 4 must be returned to the employer within three days of the date that the employee receives the form.

–The employer returns Part 3 to the IRS *(after completing the reverse side)* and keeps Part 4.

–Part 5 is the employee's copy of the tax filing status and exemption information.

» The IRS retains Part 6.

Priority vs. other attachment orders. Tax levies must be satisfied before all other garnishment or attachment orders, except for child support withholding orders in effect before the date of the levy. If more than one jurisdiction has levied on an employee's wages and there are insufficient nonexempt funds to satisfy all of them, the one received first by the employer must be satisfied before any others, unless the IRS instructs otherwise.

Figuring the amount to deduct and remit. Federal tax levies are not governed by the exemption rules that apply to garnishments or child support withholding orders under the Consumer Credit Protection Act. All amounts paid to an employee are subject to levy unless specifically exempt under the Internal Revenue Code or IRS regulations. Following is a list of payments that are exempt:

» Unemployment compensation benefits;

» Workers' compensation benefits;

» Annuity and pension payments under the Railroad Retirement Tax Act and to certain armed services personnel;

» Certain armed service-connected disability payments;

» Certain public assistance payments (welfare and supplemental social security benefits); and

» Amounts ordered withheld under a previously issued court order for child support.

In addition, each employee is entitled to an amount exempt from levy equal to the employee's standard deduction (based on Form 1040 tax filing status) and personal exemptions-including one for the employee-divided by the number of pay periods in the year. Employees paid on a daily basis have their standard deduction and personal exemption amounts divided by 260 *(52 weeks x 5 workdays per week)*. Employees who are paid on a one-time basis or on a recurrent, but irregular basis *(not the employer's regular payroll period)* are entitled to the weekly exempt amount for each week to which the payment is attributable.

The value of the employee's standard deduction and personal exemptions is determined for the year the levy is received. If the employee does not submit a verified, written statement regarding the employee's tax filing status and personal exemptions *(such as Parts 3 & 4 of Form 668-W)*, the employer must figure the exempt amount based on married filing separately with one personal exemption.

You cannot rely on the employee's Form W-4. Each year the IRS issues Publication 1494 with the tables for calculating the exempt amounts. The tables are enclosed with each notice of levy.

> »BE CAREFUL OF LEVIES SPANNING MORE THAN ONE YEAR. If the total levy cannot be collected during a calendar year, the employee must determine which year's table to use. If the employee does not complete a new Part # of Form 668-W, the employee must continue to use the table for the year during which the levy notice was received. The employee can complete a new Part 3 even if their tax filed status or number of exemptions has not changed, in order to take advantage of higher exempt amounts in the new year's tables.

Exempt amount subtracted from "take-home" pay. The amount of an employee's wages that is subject to the federal tax levy is the amount remaining after the exempt amount has been subtracted from the employee's "take-home pay". The following items may be subtracted from an employee's gross wages when calculating take-home pay:

> »Federal, state, and local taxes, even if the amounts increase while the levy is in effect due to salary or tax rate increases or changes in the employee's Form W-4;

> »Involuntary and voluntary deductions in effect before the employer received the levy, including child support withholding orders and other garnishments, elective deferrals, health and life insurance premiums, charitable donations, etc.

> »Increases in preexisting deductions beyond the employee's control, including those caused by increases in the employee's pay, such as elective deferrals of a certain percentage of salary, and those caused by increases in the cost of benefits (but not including voluntary decisions to increase the deferral percentage or to change the type of coverage provided); and

> »Deductions instituted after the levy is received and made as a condition of employment, such as a required deduction for union dues in a union shop environment.

Direct deposit is not a deduction

New voluntary deductions come from exempt amount. Any payroll deductions initiated by the employee after the employer has received the levy must be deducted from the exempt amount when determining the employee's net pay, unless they are required as a condition of employment.

Employee has two jobs; only one employer receives levy notice. Where an employee receives wages from more than one employer and only one receives a notice of levy, the employer must determine the exempt amount in the usual way unless the IRS notifies the employer that the exempt amount should be reduced because the other wages are not subject to levy.

When and where to make payments of withheld amounts. Form 668-W instructs employers to remit amounts withheld for levy on the same day wages are paid to the employee. The first payment to the IRS should accompany Part 3 of the form, after both the employer and employee complete the information requested. Payments should be sent to the IRS at the address shown on the front of Part 1. Withholding and remittance must begin with the first payment of wages to the employee after the employer receives Form 668-W, regardless of when the wages were earned. The check made payable to the IRS should have the employee's name and social security number on its face.

When to stop withholding. The employer must continue to withhold and may levy payments until it receives Form 668-D, *Release of Levy/Release of Property from Levy.* The employer cannot stop withholding when the payments match the total due stated on Part 1 of Form 668-W because interest and possible penalties continue to accumulate on the amount remaining due after each levy payment is made.

Form 668-D will contain the final amount due and release the employee's wages from levy after that amount is paid. The employer or employee should contact the IRS if Form 668-D has not been received and the total face amount due has been withheld and paid.

Procedure when employment ends. If the employee named on Form 668-W is no longer employed by the employer when the form is received, the employer must note that on the reverse side of Part 3 and return it to the IRS, along with the employee's last known address. If employment terminates while the levy is in effect, the employer should notify the IRS office where payments have been sent of the terminations and the name and address of the employee's new employer, if known. The employer must deduct and remit any nonexempt amounts contained in severance or dismissal pay provided the employee.

Employer not liable to employee for amounts withheld and remitted to the IRS in response to Form 668-W.

Penalties for failing to withhold and remit. Employers failing to withhold and remit amounts not exempt from levy after receiving Form 668-W are liable for the full amount required to be withheld, plus interest from the wage payment date. Any amount paid by the employer as a penalty will be credited against the taxes owed by the employee. In addition, the employer is liable for a penalty equal to 50% of the amount recoverable by the IRS after the failure to withhold and remit. This penalty is not applicable where there is a genuine dispute as to the amount to be withheld and paid over or the legal sufficiency of the levy.

Voluntary deduction agreement may prevent levy. An employee who owes federal taxes may be able to avoid the imposition of a federal tax levy through a "Payroll Deduction Agreement". Under such an agreement, the employee and the IRS agree that a certain amount of federal taxes is owed and that the employee's employer will deduct an amount from the employee's wages each pay period and pay it over to the IRS until full payment is made. The agreement is carried out by having the employee fill out Form 2159, *Payroll Deduction Agreement.* If the employer agrees to participate, it will sign the agreement and begin deducting and remitting to the IRS.

Child Support Withholding Orders

Since January 1, 1994, all initial orders for child support require wage withholding unless both parents or the court and one parent agree to a different method of payment. Even if such an agreement is reached, wage withholding will become automatic once the noncustodial parent owing the child support is one month late in paying support. Under the Personal Responsibility and Work Opportunity Reconciliation Act of 1996, state laws must provide that all child support orders issued or modified before October 1, 1996 that were not subject to withholding on that date, will become subject to income withholding immediately once child support payments are overdue, without the need for a court or administrative hearing.

> »Child support enforcement framework. Enforcement of child support orders is a joint federal/state responsibility, with federal laws providing standards state laws must meet or exceed in order to qualify for federal funding of state child support enforcement programs. These state standards are contained in Part D of Title IV of the Social Security Act. Title IV-D and the Consumer Credit Protection Act provide the legal framework around which state child support withholding laws are constructed.

> »The federal requirements, along with any allowable state variations, are explained in the following paragraphs:

> »*Maximum amount to withhold.* Under the CCPA, the maximum amount that can be withheld from an employee's wages for spousal or child support is:

> > –50% of the employee's "disposable earnings" if the employee is supporting another spouse and/or children; and

> > –60% if the employee is not supporting another spouse and/or children.

These amounts increase to 55% and 65%, respectively, if the employee is at least 12 weeks in arrears in making support payments. If arrearages are being paid, the total of the current support and the arrearages cannot exceed the applicable maximum amount.

» *Calculating disposable earnings.* Disposable earnings are determined by subtracting all deductions required by law from an employee's gross earnings. Voluntary deductions are not subtracted from earnings to calculate disposable earnings. Wages already subject to withholding for tax levies, bankruptcy orders, other child support withholding orders, or wage garnishments are not considered deductions by law. However, if the tax levy, bankruptcy order, etc. has priority over the current child support withholding order, the amount to be deducted under the order having priority must be taken into account when determining whether the CCPA maximum has been reached.

–TIPS MAY OR MAY NOT BE EARNINGS. Tips given directly to employees by customers are not considered earnings, whereas service charges added to the bill and later given to the employee are earnings. Check the state laws.

» *Priority of withholding orders.* Orders to withhold wages for child support take priority over all other garnishments or attachments except for tax levies received by the employer before the child support withholding order or bankruptcy court orders (they generally include amounts to satisfy child support obligations).

» *When order takes effect.* The employer must put the wage withholding order into effect no later than the first pay period beginning after 14 working days following the mailing of the notice to withhold to the employer. States may require that the order take effect sooner. Withholding must continue until the employer receives notification in writing from the court or agency involved.

» *Uniform notice to withhold.* Employers should be seeing a standard form *Order Notice to Withhold Income for Child Support* in many of their withholding situations.

» *Time to remit payment.* The employer must send payment of the withheld wages to the party noted on the withholding notice within 7 business days of the date wages are paid to the employee. State law may set a shorter time limit. Timeliness is determined by the postmark if mailed, or the date that the transmission is proven to have been initiated for electronic payments.

» *Where payment is to be made.* All states are required to have a "state disbursement unit" for the collection and disbursement of child support payments in all Title IV-D cases and in all other cases in which a child support order is issued on or after January 1, 1994. Employers send wages withheld for child support to the unit for payment to the custodial parent. Disbursement from the state disbursement unit must be made within 2 business days of their receipt from an employer if there is enough information to identify the payee.

» *Combining payments from several employees.* The employer may send one check each pay period to cover all child support withholdings if they are all to be sent to the same withholding agency and the employer separately itemizes the amount withheld from each employee and notes the date each amount was withheld. State restrictions may be more severe. Some states also allow or require the use of electronic funds transfer to make payments.

» *No discharge because of withholding.* The employer is prohibited from discharging, disciplining, or otherwise discriminating against an employee because the employee's wages are subject to withholding for child support. Violators can be fined an amount set by state law.

» *Administrative fees for employers.* Employers may charge the employee an administrative fee for processing the order each pay. The maximum amount is set by state law, and the fee must be withheld from the employee's other wages.

» *Notification after employee leaves employment.* If the employee separates from employment, the employer has a certain amount of time set by state law to notify the child support enforcement agency of the employee's last known address and, if known, the name and address of the employee's new employer. If the employee has been injured or is ill and cannot work, the employer should notify the court or agency and tell them the name and address of the entity paying workers' comp or disability benefits.

» *Penalty for not withholding.* If the employer fails to withhold the amount required by the withholding order (up to the legal maximum), it is liable for the full amount not withheld and any fine set by state law.

» Enforcement of withholding orders from other states. In 1993, an interstate commission adopted a model law to address issues of orders from other states than the one the employee works in—the Uniform Interstate Family Support Act (UIFSA). Under UIFSA an employee must put into effect a child support withholding order that it receives directly from another state's child support enforcement agency so long as the order appears "regular on its face".

» State laws adopt UIFSA. All the states adopted UIFSA by mid-1998.

» Automated data processing. Federal law requires the states to develop automated data processing systems that can manage the state's child support program, including a state case registry, and receive amounts withheld for child support and accompanying accounting information by electronic means.

Benefits of electronic payments:
» Benefits to employers:

–reduce (and eventually eliminate) manual effort required to pass child support withholding information from the payroll system to accounts payable for processing checks to CSE agencies and/or courts;

–reduce the cost of processing per item by $.15 - $.50, plus the cost savings from less manual effort, because of the lower cost of ACH processing vs. check processing, reduced account reconciliation charges, etc.;

–reduce the time and effort spent replacing lost checks and tracing mispostings.

» Benefits to financial institutions:

–opportunity for additional business with the offering of a new service to child support agencies and courts;

–conversion of prior check processing to more efficient ACH processing at no added cost.

» Benefits to CSE agency and custodial parents:

–ability to move to a more efficient electronic method of posting payments to accounts and to increase accuracy and cost effectiveness of posting payments;

–faster receipt of child support payments by custodial parents, which reduces complaints and time spent researching lost payments;

–added security and convenience of direct deposit of child support payments into custodial parents' accounts.

Complying with more than one withholding order. If an employer receives more than one child support withholding order for an employee, state law governs how they must be handled. If the orders are from different states, the law in the state where the employee works applies. These considerations generally come into play when the total withholding amount required under all orders exceeds the maximum allowed under the applicable state law.

Handling employee complaints. The employer is obligated to continue withholding according to a valid withholding order unless it receives notification in writing from the agency or court issuing the order that a change is necessary.

Employee attempts to avoid withholding. If an employee decreases the number of withholding allowances claimed, the employer should not question the employee's choice, and it is not obligated to bring it to the attention of the agency issuing the child support order.

Employers must withhold form independent contractors.

Collecting arrearages. Current support obligations must be paid before any past due amounts.

Medical child support orders. Many states have passed laws allowing courts to require medical child support as part of a child support order and requiring employers to enroll children and withhold premiums form the employees; pay to the same extent as other employees with similar coverage. New child support orders issued by a state child support agency must include a medical support provision. Medical child support orders must specify:

> »the name and address of the noncustodial parent;

> »the name and address of any children to be covered by the order;

> »a description of the coverage each child must be provided, or the way in which it will be determined;

> »the length of time coverage must be provided; and

> »each plan governed by the order.

Creditor Garnishments

Child support withholding orders are just one type of "garnishment" of an employee's wages. When an employee (debtor or obligor) has a debt that remains unpaid, a wage garnishment is one legal means by which the person who is owed the money (creditor or obligee) can obtain payment. This method requires that the employee's employer withhold the unpaid amount from the employee's wages. In some states, a wage garnishment is known as a "wage attachment" or "income execution".

> »The employer can be required to withhold a portion of the employee's wages for a wage garnishment only if the creditor first brings a court proceeding where proof of the debt is offered and the employee has a chance to respond.

> »Federal law limits garnishment amount and employee terminations. The federal Consumer Credit Protection

Act (Title III) places restrictions on states in their regulation of creditor garnishments, both:

–On the amount that may be garnished; and

–On the freedom to discharge and employee because the employee's wages have been garnished.

» *Limit on amount that can be garnished.* The CCPA states that the maximum amount of an employee's "disposable earnings" that can be garnished to repay a debt is the lesser of:

–25% of the employee's disposable earnings for the week; or

–The amount by which the employee's disposable earnings for the week exceed 30 times the federal minimum hourly wage then in effect.

–STATE LAWS MAY STILL APPLY. The garnishment limits in the CCPA preempt state laws to the extent the state laws allow greater amounts to be garnished. But state law will apply if the maximum amount subject to garnishment is lower than the federal maximum or if the state does not allow creditor garnishments at all.

Disposable earnings are determined by subtracting all deductions required by law from an employee's gross earnings (wages, commissions, bonuses, sick pay, and periodic pension payments). Voluntary deductions, such as health and life insurance premiums, union dues, and retirement plan contributions, are generally not subtracted from earnings to calculate disposable earnings. In some states, health insurance contributions may be included in the calculation of disposable pay, especially if the contributions are mandated under a child support order.

–TIPS MAY OR MAY NOT BE EARNINGS. Tips given directly to employees by customers are not considered earnings, whereas service charges added to the bill and later give to the employee are earnings. Check the state laws.

–WATCH OUT FOR MINIMUM WAGE CHANGES

» *Limit applies to multiple garnishments.*

» *Exceptions for other types of garnishments.* In determining an employee's disposable earnings, wages already subject to withholding for child support, tax levies, or bankruptcy orders are not considered deductions required by law. Therefore, they should not be subtracted from gross earnings when determining the maximum amount subject to garnishment. However, if the child support withholding order, tax levy, or bankruptcy order has priority over the creditor garnishment and constitutes at least 25% of the employee's disposable wages, no amount can be withheld for the creditor garnishment.

»Areas of state regulation. The states have a great
deal of latitude in the following areas:

–The priority of multiple garnishments;

–Whether the employer must continue to withhold
if the full amount stated in the garnishment
order exceeds the maximum that can be
withheld from the first payment of wages;

–Time limits for remitting withheld amounts;

–Whether the employer can charge an administrative
fee for processing the garnishment;

–The procedure to follow when an out-of-state
garnishment order is received; and

–Penalties for failure to withhold and remit
according to the garnishment order.

Employer's responsibilities. When an employer receives a garnishment
order from a court or government agency, it is bound to comply with the
order to withhold and remit the amount demanded, up to the maximum allowed by law. While preparing to comply, the employer should:

»Check to make sure the underlying claim is valid
and the amount stated on the order is correct by
contacting the agency or court issuing the order;

»Tell the employee about the garnishment order to make
sure the employee has received a notice that garnishment
would be taking place and has had the chance to object;

»Tell the employee about any exemptions that
might apply under state or federal law;

»Tell the employee how the garnishment will
affect his or her wages and net pay;

»Determine whether the amount demanded in the garnishment
exceeds the maximum allowed by federal or state law;

»If the employee is already subject to one or more garnishment
orders, determine their order of priority and how the
available disposable earnings must be allocated; and

»Contact legal counsel to review the garnishment order and
answer any outstanding questions regarding validity,
disposable earning determinations, complying with
out-of-state orders, priorities and allocation, etc.

Bankruptcy Orders

Bankruptcy is governed by the federal Bankruptcy Act. Once an employee voluntarily declares bankruptcy or is found to be bankrupt by a court, the satisfaction of the employee's creditors is handled by the "bankruptcy trustee" appointed by the court. Once the employee's employer receives a bankruptcy order from the trustee under a court-approved plan requiring a certain amount of the employee's wages to be paid to the trustee to satisfy the employee's creditors, the employer must stop withholding on any other garnishments against the employee.

> »Bankruptcy orders issued under Chapter XIII of the Bankruptcy Act take priority over any other claim against the employee's wages, including federal and state tax levies and child support withholding orders received **before** the bankruptcy order. (Once a bankruptcy order is received the debts underlying those garnishments will be paid by the trustee out of the money withheld under the bankruptcy order. The only time the employer should continue to withhold for other garnishments is if the trustee specifically provides instructions to do so. If the creditor is not listed in the bankruptcy order, verify with the trustee before stopping the garnishment.

Student Loan Collections

In 1991 Congress amended the Higher Education Act to allow for garnishment of employee's wages to repay delinquent student loans granted under the Federal Family Education Loan Program subject to the following restrictions:

Maximum amount subject to garnishment. If the garnishment is issued by a state guarantee agency, no more than the lesser of 10% of an employee's disposable earnings or the excess of the employee's disposable earnings over 30 times the federal hourly minimum wage then in effect may be garnished to satisfy a delinquent student loan unless the employee consents in writing to a higher percentage. However, if the Department of Education issues a garnishment order to collect on an overdue federal student loan, the maximum that can be garnished is the lesser of 15% of the employee's disposable earnings or the excess of the employee's disposable earnings over 30 times the federal hourly minimum wage then in effect.

Even though the Higher Education Act limits garnishments to 10% of an employee's wages, this limit applies to each individual holder of a student loan. Where an employee faces multiple student loan garnishments, the maximum amount that can be garnished in total is the CCPA limit of 25% of disposable earnings or the excess of the employee's weekly disposable earnings above 30 times the federal minimum hourly wage, whichever is less.

> »**Notice before garnishment**. Employees must receive at least 30 days' notice before withholding begins and must be given a chance to work out a repayment schedule with the agency guaranteeing the loan to avoid garnishment.

»No guidance on priorities. The amendments provide no guidance on priorities, however the Department of Education has allowed child support withholding orders to take priority.

»**Grace period after reemployment.** Employees who lose their jobs and become reemployed within 12 months after termination are given 12 months from their date of reemployment before a student loan garnishment order can be put into effect.

»Penalties for noncompliance. If the employer fails to comply with a lawful student loan garnishment order, it is liable for the amount not withheld as well as other costs and damages.

Federal Agency Debt Collections

In 1996 Congress enacted the Debt Collection Improvement Act which allows federal government agencies that administer a program under which they provide money to individuals to garnish the wages of individuals who fail to repay their dept according to their agreement with the agency. These garnishments can only be applied to nontax debts (tax debts are collected through tax levies issued by the IRS). This law preempts state laws governing garnishments.

Maximum amount subject to garnishment. CCPA as well as the Debt Collection Improvement Act limit the maximum. The amount to be garnished is the lesser of:

»The amount indicated on the garnishment order up to 15% of the employee's disposable pay, or

»The amount by which the employee's disposable pay exceeds 30 times the federal minimum hourly wage then in effect.

Where an employee owes multiple debts to one federal agency, the agency may issue multiple withholding orders for the debts, so long as the total amount garnished does not exceed the limit for one garnishment.

»Employers are required to certify information about the employee's employment status and disposable pay (defined as amounts required to be deducted by law and to pay for health insurance) on a form accompanying the withholding order and to pay over amounts withheld "promptly" after payday.

»Notice before garnishment. Employees must receive notice of a federal agency garnishment before withholding is to begin and must be given a chance to contest the garnishment or work out a voluntary repayment schedule.

»**Priority of multiple withholding orders.** Unless otherwise provided by federal law, federal agency wage garnishments have priority over other types of withholding orders served on the employer after the federal agency wage garnishment, except for family support orders. If an employee's pay is already subject to another type of withholding order, or if a family support withholding order is served at any time, the amount subject to the federal agency wage garnishment is the lesser of:

–The amount indicated on the garnishment order up to 15% of the employee's disposable pay, or the amount by which the employee's disposable pay exceeds 30 times the federal minimum hourly wage then in effect, or

–25% of the employee's disposable pay minus the amounts withheld under the withholding orders with priority.

» **Grace period after reemployment.** Employees who lose their jobs involuntarily are given 12 months from their date of reemployment before a federal agency loan garnishment order can be put into effect. The employee must notify the agency of his or her involuntary termination.

» **Penalties for noncompliance.** If the employer fails to comply with a lawful federal agency loan garnishment order, it is liable for the amount not withheld as well as other costs and damages.

Federal Wage-Hour Law Restrictions on Deductions

The Fair Labor Standards Act, also known as the Federal Wage-Hour Law, places its own restrictions on deductions when they bring an employee's wages below the minimum wage and overtime pay guaranteed by the Act.

Voluntary Deductions

Wage Assignments

A wage assignment is a voluntary agreement by an employee (assignor) to have a portion of the employee's wages assigned to a third party (assignee). Generally, the employees assign wages to secure a debt. The assignment gives the creditor an opportunity to recover the unpaid amount if the employee fails to repay the debt. Sometimes an assignment will be used to pay the debt directly, rather than waiting for the employee to default. And in some cases, noncustodial parents may be allowed to voluntarily assign a portion of their wages to pay child support rather than having to submit to a child support withholding order.

Garnishment limits do not apply. Voluntary wage assignments are not covered by CCPA.

State law governs wage assignments.

Union Dues

In addition to mandatory deductions for union dues required by a collective bargaining agreement in some situations employees have the option of paying union dues on their own or having them deducted from their wages by their employer. This voluntary check-off procedure is authorized by federal law (Labor Management Relations Act), so long as the amount withheld is for union dues, initiation fees, and assessment only.

Credit Union Deductions

Employers often encourage the formation and use of credit unions by agreeing to the payroll deductions.

U.S. Savings Bonds

Employees can purchase Series EE U.S. Savings Bonds in denominations beginning at $100. The purchase price of the bond is one-half of the bond's denomination or "face value".

»**Interest accumulation.** Interest begins to accumulate in the month during which the party issuing the bond receives payments for the bond. Interest accrues at various rates depending on the length the bond is held. The bonds mature at 12 years.

»**Tax advantages for the employee.** Interest earned on Series EE bonds is free from federal income tax until the bond is redeemed. The interest may be totally tax-free if the bond is used to finance the college education of the employee's children. The interest is also not taxable at the state or local level.

»**Authorization procedures.** The employer supplies enrollment cards, and they can be obtained from any regional office of the U.S. Treasury Department.

»**Employer responsibilities.** Employers must make sure the proper amounts have been deducted and remitted by reconciling the deductions and the bonds purchased. And they must return any excess amounts deducted to the employees or use them toward the purchase of more bonds.

»**Administration of the program.** Employers can choose how involved they wish to get in the administration of the payroll deduction program. They can become "issuing agents" who draft the bonds and give them to employees as they are purchased, or they can provide enrollment data and payment for the bonds to a third-party administrator, Federal Reserve Bank, or other depository institution that issues the bonds. When acting as an issuing agent, the employer is paid an administrative fee based on the number of bonds issued.

Charitable Contributions

Section 13172 of the Omnibus Budget Reconciliation Act of 1993 prohibits taxpayers from deducting charitable contributions of $250 or more without substantiation of the gift and any substantial goods or services received in return. The required substantiation is a "contemporaneous written acknowledgement" (before the taxpayer files his or her personal tax return for the year of the contribution) from the charitable organization that includes the following information:

> » The amount of cash and a description of any noncash property contributed,

> » Whether the charitable organization provided any goods or services in return for the contribution, and

> » A description and good faith estimate of the value of these goods or services.

Employer and charity share reporting burden. The regulations allow employees to substantiate contributions by a combination of two documents:

> » A pay stub, Form W-2, or other document provided by the employer that shows the amount withheld for payment to a charitable organization, and

> » A pledge card or other document prepared by the charitable organization or another party (e.g., the employer) at the direction of the charitable organization that includes a statement that no goods or services are provided in return for employee contributions made by payroll deduction.

$250 threshold applies separately to each deduction. The amount withheld from each wage payment to an employee is treated as a separate contribution. Thus, the substantiation requirements do not apply unless the employer withholds at least $250 from a single paycheck for purposes of paying it to a charitable organization.

CHAPTER 10

Record Retention

Compliance with the various federal, state, and local laws affecting payroll is impossible without keeping accurate records for each employee. While different laws may require the gathering and processing of different types of records and retention by the employer for varying lengths of time, the failure to maintain the proper records can be quite costly in terms of noncompliance penalties as well as penalties for violating the recordkeeping requirements themselves. Below is a quick reference of the record retention requirements of each type of payroll document.

» Time Sheets 2 years

» FLSA/IRCA/FMLA :3 years and available within 72 hours

- Name of employee/address/occupation/birth date

- Hours worked each day/week (or basis for compensation for exempts)

- Amount and date of payment (including tips and tip credit used)

- Amounts earned for straight time and overtime pay

- Collective bargaining agreements

- Sales and purchase records

- Immigration Reform and Control Act (IRCA)

- Form I-9 (3yrs after hire or 1 year after term whichever is longer)

- Dates/hours of FMLA leave

- Copies of request/notices/disputes over FMLA

»IRS/SSA/FUTA documents—4 years

–Duplicate copies of tax returns/tax deposits

–Returned copies of W-2's

–Canceled/voided checks

–Employee's name/address/occupation/security number

–Amount/date of payment for wages,
 annuities, pensions, tips, FMV's

–Health Insurance, section 125, Educational Assistance
 and Deferred Comp plan documents

–Record of allocated tips

–Amount of wages subject to withholding

–Taxes withheld (and date if different from pay date)

–Copies of Form W4 (for as long as valid and 4 years after)

–Agreements to withhold additional amounts

–Copies of 941, 940, W-2, W-3 and any
 other forms filed on magnetic tape

»OSHA documents: 5 Years

–Log of all occupational illnesses/accidents

–Other OSHA records (injury on the
 job, worker's comp claims)

CHAPTER 11

Payroll Accounting

Accounting Principles

Accounting is a way to track financial transactions by identifying & classifying transactions to be included in the preparation of financial statements. Financial statements are used by:

» Management

» Stockholders

» Auditors Accounting standards are NOT set by law. Since 1974 the Financial Accounting Standards Board (FASB) has set the standards for recording financial transactions.

Generally Accepted Accounting Principles (GAAP) were established prior to 1974. These include:

» Business entity concept

» Continuing concern concept

» Time period concept

» Cost principle

» Objectivity principle

» Matching principle

» Realization principle

» Consistency principle Account Classifications

Transactions are recorded and classified using a 'double entry' system that is based on two sets of equations. To remain in balance one account is increased while another is decreased.

The first equation:

»Assets—Liabilities = Equity *(basis for the Balance Sheet)*

The second set of equations:

»Revenue - Expenses = Net Income *(basis for Income Statement)*

»Net Income - Income Distributed + Contributed Capital = Equity *(basis for Statement of Retained Earnings)*

TYPES OF ACCOUNTS

Asset Accounts

Asset provides economic benefit/value. Three classes/types of asset accounts based on liquidity (liquidity is the ability to be converted to cash):

»**Current** (ex. Cash, Receivables, Inventory, Prepaid expenses)

»**Tangible or Property, Plant & Equipment** (ex. Land & improvements, Buildings, Computers & Software, Furniture, Automobiles)

»**Intangible or Deferred** (ex. Trademarks, Patents, Leases, Goodwill, Copyrights)

Expense Accounts

Expenses are the costs for goods & services consumed during the period. Examples of expenses:

»Wages paid to employees

»Employer paid benefit costs

»Maintenance for computers

»Office supplies

»Employer share of payroll taxes

Liability Accounts

Liabilities are debts that must be paid—represent a claim against assets) Two categories: Current and Long Term. Liabilities classed as current must be paid within the accounting period (fiscal year). Long term liabilities can be paid after the current period (fiscal year). Examples of liabilities:

»Income and employment taxes withheld but not yet deposited

»Contributions owed to a company benefit plan

»Accounts payable

»Wages payable

»Union dues deducted from employee's pay but not yet paid to the union

Revenue Accounts

Revenue is the amount received for goods sold or services provided during the accounting period—can be cash, expectation of receiving cash, or services.

Equity Accounts

Equity represents the owner's investment in the company. Two components of equity = Contributed Capital and Retained Earnings.

ACCOUNT BALANCES

Each type of account has what is called a normal balance on one side of the equation. With the double entry system each entry is always in balance and all entries are always in balance.

Debits, Credits, "T-accounts"—The basic manual process of recording transactions helps to clarify the understanding. A "T-account" looks like the letter T with the DEBIT portion of the entry recorded on the left and the CREDIT portion of the entry recorded on the right

»DEBIT = LEFT SIDE OF T ACCOUNT

»CREDIT = RIGHT SIDE OF T ACCOUNT

Posting entries

It is important to know the normal account balance for each type of account!!

If an account has a normal debit balance an entry that increases the account is a debit and an entry that decreases the account is a credit.

If an account has a normal credit balance an entry that increases the account is a credit and an entry that decreases the account is a debit.

Unit of measurement

US businesses record in US dollars

Chart of accounts

Lists each account by name & number with logic built into numbering scheme.

Journal Entries

Journal is a record of the transactions of a company during the accounting period. Contains both debits and credits to be entered into specific accounts and a description of the transaction.—Recording journal entries is also called journalizing into **the book of original entry**.

Compound entries
Contain more than one debit or credit

Subsidiary ledgers
Specialized journal that is summarized for posting to the general ledger (Payroll Register is a type of subsidiary ledger).

General Ledger
Entries that are recorded in journals or subsidiary ledgers are posted to the General Ledger which keeps a running total of all the entries and period-to-date balance for all accounts (**book of final entry**). The General Ledger is used to prepare the **financial statements**:

> » **Balance Sheet** provides a look at the company's financial condition at a specific point in time by listing assets, liabilities and equity.

> » **Income Statement** shows net income or loss for period— the difference between revenue and expenses

> » **Statement of Retained Earnings** shows income remaining & available for investment after stockholder (owner) distributions

> » **Statement of Cash Flows** shows sources and uses of cash during period

Recording Payroll Transactions
Payroll transactions are initially recorded in Payroll Register.

Payroll expenses may be recorded in one of two ways:
> » **Functionally**—entries must be based on the processes supported by the expenses—payroll would be distributed into different labor distribution expense accounts into a separate Labor Distribution Subsidiary Ledger with the total agreeing to gross pay total in payroll register.

> » **By Type of Pay**—breaks wages down into regular and overtime pay

Payroll deductions
Employer liability incurred on the date that the deduction is made from employee wages.

Payroll cash distribution / net pay
When the employees are paid, the payroll checking account is credited and the accrued salaries/wages liability account is debited.

Employer tax liabilities

The employer tax expenses (OASDI, Medicare, FUI, SUI) are initially debited to an expense account and credited to a liability account. When the taxes are paid, the liability account is debited and the cash account is credited.

Accounting Periods

The IRS does not require businesses to use the calendar year as their accounting year. Any 12 month accounting period can be adopted by a business for their accounting year *(fiscal year)*.

An accounting period is any length of time covered by an income statement (month, quarter, half-year, year). Regardless of the accounting periods or fiscal year adopted by a business **PAYROLL TAXES ARE ALWAYS REPORTED ON A CALENDAR YEAR BASIS.**

Accruals and Reversals

Accrual method accounting recognizes revenue when earned and expenses when incurred. IRS accepts both cash and accrual methods. GAAP accepts only accrual. Accrual satisfies Matching Principle which requires revenue, expenses & liabilities to be matched to the period in which they are earned or incurred.

Accruals are estimates and must be reversed during the following period when actual expenses & liabilities are recorded.

Vacations

Vacation time is accrued as earned (DB expense, CR liability)

Bonuses

Nondiscretionary bonuses are accrued when earned *(DB expense, CR liability)*.

Balancing and Reconciling Payroll Accounts

»Balancing / Reconciling should be done to ensure accuracy.

»General ledger accounts should be compared to records of taxes withheld and paid.

»Verify tax amounts on general ledger to payroll register records

»Verify checks issued by accounts payable have been posted to correct accounts.

»Verify end-of-month balances for tax accounts agree with payroll records.

117

Periodic Balancing and Reconciliation

Every pay period—verify the following from pay register record:
»Gross wages less deductions equals net amount payable

»Total amount of withheld OASDI & Medicare equals the current rate multiplied by total taxable wages for the period

»Other payroll taxes / taxable wages should be checked for reasonableness

»Ensure there are no missing paychecks

Before filing Forms 941 and 940—verify the following:
»OASDI & Medicare tax deposits for the QTR equal the current tax rates for each multiplied by total taxable wages for each

»Total tax deposits for the QTR equal the number in the liability section of Form 941 (Exception: monthly depositors may pay any lawful deposit shortfalls with Qtrly Form 941; therefore total tax deposits for the QTR may not equal total liability if taking advantage of 98% safe harbor.)

»Total gross wages on Line 1 of Form 940 can be reconciled with total on Line 2 of the four Qtrly Forms 941 filed for the year. May not be equal but MUST be reconciled.

Before sending employees W-2 forms—verify the following:
»Total amounts of withheld taxes and OASDI & Medicare taxable wages reported on Qtrly Forms 941 EQUAL total of all Forms W-2 being issued.

»Total wages reported on Line 2 of Form 941 need not equal Box 1—not required by IRS—but must be reconciled to explain differences.

Payroll Bank Account Reconciliation

Internal and external auditors recommend that employees who issue or control checks on an account should not be responsible for reconciliation of that account. Someone outside of payroll dept should reconcile payroll bank account.

Differences typically are attributed to checks not yet cashed; deposits not yet credited; or bank charges

Reconciliation is made simpler by direct deposit.

Checks not cashed—must be tracked & investigated. Uncashed / unclaimed checks become unclaimed wages and subject to state's escheat laws.

Financial Statements & Audits

Payroll data significantly impacts financial statements. Poor or inaccurate payrolls can materially misrepresent a company's financial condition.

Balance Sheet

Assets listed first, followed by liabilities and finally equity *(net worth)*

> »Current assets
>
> »Plant, property, and equipment
>
> »Deferred assets
>
> »Current liabilities
>
> »Long-term liabilities
>
> »Shareholders' equity (net worth)

Income Statement

Summarizes revenues & expenses and determines earnings for the current and preceding fiscal years.

Gross margin on sales
Net sales *(sales less returns & discounts)* minus cost of goods sold *(excluding overhead, taxes, or revenue not generated by sales)*.

Operating income *(operating profit)*
Takes into consideration overhead but not taxes or nonoperating revenues/expenses.

Nonoperating revenue
revenue not generated by sales *(ex interest or capital gains)*

Nonoperating expenses
Includes interest expense & income taxes

Net earnings (net income/loss)
Bottom line—profit/loss after paying taxes

Earnings per share
Net earnings divided by average number of outstanding shares of stock during the accounting period.

Notes To Financial Statements

Explanations of accounting policies that have major impact on financial statements. Changes in procedures disclosed. Benefit plans vesting & accruals disclosure.

Auditing Financial Statements

Independent CPAs determine if statements adequately & accurately depict company's financial condition.

Auditors & Payroll Dept

Review of dept for accuracy of records and soundness of practices/ policies/ procedures.

> »Compliance test on sample of cancelled paychecks & supporting information *(time cards, W-4, payroll register, deduction authorizations, calculations)*

> »Review of processing procedures and payroll data input—separation of duties

> »Blank check storage

> »Check distribution—may conduct physical payout to protect against phantom employees

Internal Controls

Checks and balances to ensure accuracy of financial records & security of assets. Internal controls encourage employees to comply with company policies/procedures. Basic components of internal controls:

> »Segregation of job duties

> »Rotation of job duties

> »Payroll distribution

> »Phantom employees

> »Negative pay deductions

> »Payroll bank account

> »Blank checks

> »Time reporting

> »Computer system edits

> »Using an internal auditor

Controlling Check Fraud

Group 1 security

Manufactured into the check paper; difficult & expensive to reproduce

> »Mould made and fourdriner watermarks
>
> »Overt fibers and planchettes
>
> »Covert fibers
>
> »Chemical reactants
>
> »Toner Bond Enhancers

Group 2 security

Printed onto the paper either when paper is converted from raw material to check stock or when MICR or OCR lines, payee, or amount info is completed. Combines design & ink to defeat some type of tampering.

> »Screened printing
>
> »Micro printing
>
> »Simulated watermarks
>
> »Warning bands and security icons
>
> »VOID features
>
> »Prismatic Printing
>
> »Anti-splice lines
>
> »Aniline Dye
>
> »Holograms and foils
>
> »Thermonth chromic ink
>
> »Nonnegotiable backer
>
> »Security lock icons and descriptions

Group 3 security

"Positive Pay" bank sponsored electronic data checking. ***Most effective security measure***, also most costly & labor intensive. Requires one-to-one comparison of check info with company and bank records.

Positive Pay requires verification of check number and check value before the check is processed.

Training bank personnel in detection is a problem—nonexistent or poor training defeats the effectiveness of most Group 1 and 2 security features.

CHAPTER 12

Payroll Systems

Objectives of a Computerized Payroll System

A payroll system must meet the needs of the payroll department's customers which include:

» The employees it pays;

» Other departments in the company;

» The company's upper management; and

» The federal, state, and local government agencies to whom withheld income and employment taxes, child support payments, etc. are paid and reported.

A successful payroll system must:

» Provide for compliance with federal, state, and local withholding, depositing, and reporting requirements.

» Issue timely and accurate paychecks, direct deposits and other disbursements.

» Maintain adequate records of all data and transactions.

» Prepare internal reports

» Guarantee the security of the system.

Interfacing and Integration

Payroll and human resources, along with benefits, control nearly all employee-related data.

In many companies, this has led to integration of the payroll and human resources system *(and sometimes benefits as well)* into one shared database. In others, the two departments transfer data from one system to the other and to other company systems as well through interfaces.

Interfacing-Working With Other Systems and Departments

The place where two systems meet is called the interface. When two systems are interfaced, they can talk to each other and be understood, sharing data needed by both. If information needed by more than one system can be used by each system after being entered only once, the cost of entering, need for verification, and chances for data entry errors are greatly reduced.

The following internal and external systems generally require a direct interface with the payroll system and benefit the most from a fully automated linkage.

» Human resources

» Benefits

» Labor cost data collection

» Payroll bank accounts

» Direct deposit/EFT

» Time and attendance

» Accounts payable

» General ledger/cost accounting

» Outside benefit plan administrators

» Social Security Administration

» State unemployment insurance

» Tax deposits

Integration of Payroll and Human Resource Systems

In recent years, an increasing number of companies have implemented Integrated Human Resource Management Systems (IHRMS) that provide a shared database for human resources, payroll, and benefits information.

An integrated system does the following:

» Eliminates double data entry;

» Makes better use of available staff;

» Eliminates timing issues; and

»Greatly reduces data discrepancies.

Reasons for integration.
Some of the more common reasons include:

»Streamlining the payroll, human resources, and benefits functions.

»The lack of complete data in any single separate database.

»Significant improvements in existing systems are often impossible because a lot of time and energy is spent supporting necessary interfaces among the existing systems and databases.

»Providing a secure database that can be the foundation for employee and/or manager self-service application.

Procedures for implementation.
When considering an IHRMS the following would need to be done to provide a basis for determining whether integration is both desirable and feasible:

»The current human resources and payroll systems would have to be analyzed;

»Current and future requirements carefully stated; and

»Goals detailed

Hardware and Software Alternatives—Pros and Cons

When considering acquisition of a new computerized payroll system the project team must decide:

»What type of computer equipment (hardware) will drive the system, and

»What kinds of programs (software) will be needed to produce the desired results

Generally there are four alternatives:
»Service bureau,

»In-house computer with custom-designed software,

»In-house computer with vendor-supplied software, and

»A combination of these elements.

Service Bureaus

A service bureau is an independent company that processes its clients' payrolls for a fee.

The hardware and software used to process the payroll belong to the service bureau, with programs being designed to meet many of the employer's needs.

The data provided to the service bureau may be sent electronically or on paper (requiring the service bureau to key the data), with paychecks, direct deposit advices, written reports, and computer files being sent to the employer in return.

The cost of using a service bureau depends largely on the volume of data to be processed and the amount of programming needed to produce the desired results.

Historically, service bureaus have been more attractive to smaller companies

In recent years, however, some larger companies have found service bureaus to be a less costly alternative to in-house processing.

Advantages of service bureau payroll processing.
»Low fixed costs

»No extra room or employees

»New services can be added

»Reduction in processing delays

»Reasonable processing costs

»Fewer research problems

»Networking possibilities

»Training and support

Disadvantages of the service bureau approach.
»Lack of control over security

»Responsibility for filing errors

»Little time for changes

»Unique needs create problems

»Possibly high variable costs

»No control over breakdowns

In-House Payroll Systems

An in-house computerized payroll system is located on company premises, whether the hardware is owned or leased by the employer.

Also, the system is operated by the employer's own employees

HARDWARE OPTIONS.

Mainframe computers

Mainframes are the largest and most powerful computers used for business, and in most companies where they are used they comprise the entire computer system.

Each department is linked to the mainframe and uses it in much the same way that a client/employer uses a time-share computer.

Minicomputers

Minicomputers are smaller and less costly than mainframes.

They may serve the same purpose as a mainframe in small and mid-size companies, with each department sharing access to the system.

They can also run a diverse variety of software that can be tailored to the payroll department's needs.

Microcomputers, or personal computers (PCs)

Microcomputers or PCs have gained great popularity in recent years as their power, speed, and capacity have increased.

They are also extremely flexible, with a great number of vendors offering many different types of software and add-on products that can be shuffled to produce the right combination for each employer.

Microcomputer networks

A network connects computers and applications.

The network consists of two basic elements, the physical connections and the software that supports the application in its interactions between the PCs and the server.

Local Area Network (LAN)

In a LAN environment, all computers are physically attached to each other and data are transmitted at high speeds over short distances.

The main computer or file server (a minicomputer or workstation) manages the LAN.

Wide Area Network (WAN)

In a WAN environment, information can be transmitted over long distances at slower transmission speeds using telephone lines.

Client/server technology—another option

Client/server is a method of network computing in which the application programs are distributed by running on a personal computer.

The data reside on a "server", which can be a mainframe, minicomputer, or workstation PC.

The payroll application itself resides on the PCs in the payroll department and is maintained by the server.

A client/server system provides a great deal of flexibility in processing.

Client/server applications are generally composed of some or all of the following elements:

» The hardware

» The graphic user interface

» The file management system

» The network operating system

» The communications protocol

There are several system configurations that meet the definition of client/server. Here are two examples:

» A simple configuration would be a PC as a server networked in a LAN to a number of other PCs as clients.

» A larger configuration might be a minicomputer as a server linked in a LAN environment to PC clients.

Data processing options
There are two alternative methods of processing payroll data on an in-house system.

» Real-time processing

» Batch processing

While batch processing is generally less expensive than real-time processing, it may not provide the immediate results that are required from a modern payroll system.

Advantages of an in-house mainframe or minicomputer system.
» Control of the system

» Convenient access

» Downtime can be reduced

» System security

» Scheduling flexibility

» Interactive applications

Disadvantages of in-house mainframe or minicomputer systems.
» Sufficient secure space needed

»High fixed costs

»Additional staffing

»Working below capacity

»System obsolescence

»Disaster recovery a must for sound business practice

»Wrong computer chosen

Advantages of in-house microcomputer (PC) networks.
While most of the same advantages provided by having an in-house mainframe or minicomputer would apply in the PC network situation, there would be other benefits as well.

»Data sharing

»Improved communications

Disadvantages of in-house microcomputer networks.
»Initial installation costs

»Network manager needed

»Upgrades needed to keep the system up to date

Software considerations for an in-house system
The software can come from three sources:

»It can be off the shelf,

»Vendor-supplied, or

»Developed and customized by the employer's own programmers

Advantages of off-the-shelf software.
»Use it right away

»Low cost

»Ease of use

»Wide variety of programs

»Yearly updates

Disadvantages of off-the-shelf software.
»PC-based only

»No modifications

»Small employers only

Advantages of vendor-supplied software packages.
»Speedy implementation

»Significant cost savings

»Vendor does the updating

»Ease of use

»User group networking

»Reduced reliance on in-house systems personnel

»Better documentation

Disadvantages of purchased software packages.
»Specific needs may not be met

»Possibly slow changes

»Extensive training needed

»Lengthy processing

»Improper fit

Advantages of customized software.
»Special needs met

»Employer has control

»Increased flexibility

»Reduced training needs

Disadvantages of customized software.
»Additional time and staff needed

»Update responsibility

»Limits on expansion

»Employees leave the company

»Poor documentation

Selecting a Computerized Payroll System

A variety of questions must be answered before a decision can be made as to what type of system to use—service bureau or in-house. The company must decide:

»Whether the system will be integrated for all employee-
related information and what interfaces with
other departments will be necessary;

»What functions must the system perform;

»Who will need access to the system;

»How the data will be processed; and

»How much money can be spent.

These questions can be answered only after receiving input from all involved users of payroll information in the company as to their needs and desires.

Build a Project Team

Because of the effect the selection decision will have on the company, the initial step is to put together a project team or task force representing all the potential end users of the system.

These departments generally include, among others:

»Payroll

»Human resources

»Benefits

»Accounting

»Tax

»Budget/finance

»Data processing/MIS

»Management

When selecting members of the project team, be sure to look for:

»Employees from other departments who have knowledge of their departments' needs regarding payroll and human resources as well as computer systems in general.

Also, make sure they:

»Can commit the time necessary to work on the system selection project,

»Their managers support their participation, and

»They will be employees who will use the new system on a daily basis.

Don't Forget Anyone

In order to make sure no area has been forgotten in selecting the project team, prepare a flowchart of the entire payroll process and determine the areas that are affected.

Analyze What the System Needs to Do

The project team's first, and maybe most important, job is to complete a thorough "needs and wants analysis".

Document the current system and its problems.
» Document the paper flow of work into the system

» Document the paper flow out of the system

» Document the procedures for maintenance of the system

» Identify who receives information from the payroll system, how often they get it, and whether they are using the information

» Have the end users identify and prioritize complaints, problems, and restrictions of the current system and analyze their cause

» Identify any actual or potential compliance problems with the current system

» Document any manual processes currently used by payroll or other departments that might be eliminated by automation.

» Identify all costs of the current system

Define the objectives you need to meet regarding the new system.
» Scope

– What do you want to accomplish

» Time

– How much time is needed to select and implement a new system?

– Is there a required date by when the new system must be functional?

» Resources

– Who will be involved in the process?

– What is the planning budget and the budget for the new system?

– What is the budget for training and support once the new system is operational?

Define the requirements a new payroll system must meet.
» What earnings and deductions calculations must be performed, and what information is needed to make those calculations?

» What internal and government reports must the system generate?

» How much more or less information should be included

on documents output from the system, and should
they be sent to more or fewer individuals?

» What integration or interfaces are required in the new system?

» What training will have to be provided?

» What will be the company's future system needs, based
on estimates of growth, resources, decentralization,
mergers, etc. and their effect on payroll processing?

» What type of support will be needed from the
system manufacturer or software vendor?

» Should the system be integrated for all employee information
used by payroll, human resources, and benefits?

It is important for the team to keep in mind any restraints that might restrict their selection; such as inadequate budgeted funds or the limitations of current hardware that will not be replaced.

Team members must prioritize their needs and desires.

Prepare a Request for Proposal

The next step is to prepare a "request for proposal" (RFP) or a "request for quotation" (RFQ). The RFP:

» Is a document that asks for bids from potential vendors
of hardware or software, as well as service bureaus?

» Should provide a detailed explanation of what the employer
wants from its system so a vendor can determine whether
its hardware or software can meet those needs or whether it
can customize its software to the employer's satisfaction.

» Can be used to help design the system if the team is moving
towards the purchase of an in-house system. The responses
from vendors can be compared for costs and services.

» Should be sufficiently detailed in defining both the technical
and functional requirements of the new system.

» Should require vendors to use a predetermined form
so their proposals can easily be compared.

» May ask for short (Yes/No) answers in a checklist, as
well as provide space for explanations if needed.

» Should include the following information about the employer:

–Purpose in issuing the proposal;

–Why a new system is needed and what has been done so far;

–Specific payroll information;

–Number of fields required for earnings and deductions;

–Functional requirements of a new system
now and in the future;

–Whether human resources and benefits will be integrated with
the payroll system and what interfaces will be required;

–Whether the vendor should include the cost of training
in the bid, taking into account the time needed, travel
if required, and number of employees to be trained;

–Level of support expected;

–Contract terms and conditions *(after review
by the legal department)*; and

–Instructions to the vendor on how to submit the proposal.

Select a System

The steps to be taken by the project team in this part of the selection process are as follows:

» Ask to see a demonstration of the vendor's products or
services at the vendor's premises and at companies
currently under contract with the vendor *(include
companies not referred by the vendor).*

» Try to schedule site demonstrations at companies
with a similar environment to the employer in
terms of industry type, size, hardware, etc.

» If the vendor claims a product and "take care of" a
situation or problem, ask for a demonstration.

» Make sure all necessary government reports and requirements
can be accomplished by the vendor's software.

» If the team is considering vendor-supplied software for an
already existing in-house computer, ask the vendor to
demonstrate the software on the employer's hardware.

Mistakes to avoid

» Failing to provide project team members time to do the job right

» Failing to include representatives of all potential
user departments on the project team

» Failing to prioritize needs and desires

» Not considering future company needs and plans

» Making decisions without sufficient input

» Failing to consider all the costs associated with a new system

» Seeing software demonstrated on different
   hardware than what you will be using

» Seeing demonstration or making reference calls only with
   companies referred by the vendor or service bureau

» Failing to negotiate performance guarantees

» Failing to thoroughly check for signs of obsolescence

» Failing to check the vendor's financial background
   and outlook for the future

Verify feasibility before making a final recommendation

Implement the System

Preparing for implementation
Clearly define the goals and requirements the new system must meet.

Make sure team members have the time to devote to the implementation part of the project.

Allow sufficient time for completion of the entire implementation and for each task involved, taking into consideration possible unforeseen problems and delays.

The project team manager must have the support and cooperation of upper management and the other team members at this crucial stage of the process.

Training team members and the payroll staff

Converting old data and adding new data
The location of the data must be identified in the old system, as must the location of the file for the data in the new system.

Test the conversion with a small, representative piece of the data before attempting to convert all the data.

After the conversion has taken place, but while the data are still in both systems, the converted data must be verified by comparing the data in each system.

There may also be new data that must be entered manually.

Testing the new system
A piecemeal approach may best serve to avoid future problems.

At first, individual processes of the software can be "unit tested" using a representative sample.

Then "system test" as a whole. This testing should include verification of the necessary interfaces, printing requirements, etc.

Make sure the system can spot errors. Test the logic built into the system.

Parallel testing

The final test before going "live" is called parallel testing.

The same data are processed by both the old and new systems

Parallels can also be run for different pay cycles and pay periods at different times during the quarter or year.

System conversion

Work flow to and from the new system must be documented and agreed on, since fewer and/or different people may be sending paperwork to or receiving paperwork from the payroll department when the new system is up and running.

It is also very important for the team to develop contingency plans for what must be done should something go wrong either during the conversion or the first pay cycle.

Evaluate the System's Performance

Even after a successful initial implementation there are problems that must be watched for, including:

> »New internal report requirements or old requirements that were missed that the system was designed to meet;

> »Unexpected legislation with payroll implications;

> »Radical changes in company benefit plans

Periodic reviews of the system should be undertaken to identify problems and prioritize their resolution.

Controls and Security for the Computerized Payroll System

The project team's final responsibility is to develop and institute procedures to make sure errors are kept to a minimum and the system and the data store there are secure.

Putting Controls Into the Process

> »System edits

> »Periodic data auditing and sampling

> »Batch controls

> »Correction procedures

> »Balancing and reconciliation

System Documentation

What to include

A confidentiality statement that emphasizes to employees the confidential nature of the manual itself as well as the employee data.

Introductions to both the manual and the system itself.

Helpful information on getting around in the system.

The "guts" of the manual will be the actual payroll or human resources processing sections, including a processing calendar.

Other important information can be brought together in an appendix.

What to leave out

»A system manual should not include company policies or technical material.

How to package the document

»Use a loose leaf binder

»Create a cover that is pleasing to the eye, using company logos and colors where available.

»Use durable, color dividers for each section.

How to keep the manual up to date

An electronic copy should be kept on the company's LAN with another on diskettes as backup.

It is also wise to keep a paper copy of each section in a file folder so written notations can be made as changes are made, which can then be keyed in to the master.

Documentation promotes control

Documentation makes it much easier for a payroll manager to rotate job assignments, and schedule reassignments due to time off.

Documentation procedures also make training of new, rotated, or newly assigned employees much easier and allow individuals to train at their own pace.

It also provides a quick reference for employees and gives internal and external auditors an accurate ideach of what should be taking place.

Providing Security for the System

Personnel concerns

»Segregation of job duties

» Rotation of job assignments

» Paychecks go only to employees

» Conduct "physical payouts"

» In small payroll departments give some payroll tasks to other departments

System security

» Limit system access

» Secure files

» Develop audit trails

» Protect against computer "viruses"

» Back up data regularly and store off site

Physical plant issues

» Climate-controlled rooms

» Keep terminals from overheating

» Do not store in cold area

» Protect against power surges

» Keep dirt out of components

» Keep the humidity down

» Check for adequate power

Disaster Recovery

» Find and secure interim office space

» Arrange office equipment rental

» Find suitable temporary housing for employees

» Keep backup files off premises

» Keep employee safety uppermost in any plans

» Communicate the plan

Automated Time and Attendance Reporting

Benefits of automation

» Labor cost reduction

» Easy to use

» Flexibility

» Managers can manage

Handling exempt employees

Some companies use the automated system only for nonexempt employees, but this cancels some cost savings.

One solution is to have a system that differentiates between the two types of employees and requires exempt employees to enter information into the system only when they are changing their schedules or taking time off. Such a system is known as "exception time collection".

The New Wave-Employee Self-Service and the Internet

Employee and Manager Self-Service

An employee self-service application gives an employee access to his or her personnel data and allows the employee to review, print out, and/or update certain portions of that data.

The most common applications so far include data updates and benefits enrollments and changes, but new uses are being added all the time, including:

» Electronic pay stubs

» Changes to withholding allowances

» Updating voluntary deduction information

» Updating direct debit information

» Helping employees calculate net pay if they make changes to withholding, etc.

» Processing requests for duplicate W-2;

Organizations that are using employee self-service applications have found that they are getting cleaner, more accurate, and more timely information at a small fraction of the cost of doing it through paper systems.

Following are several ways in which employee self-service applications can be delivered and used by employees:

Kiosks

» Specialized workstations located for easy employee access

» They generally have user-friendly touch screen capabilities

» They cannot be used by remote or mobile employees

Interactive Voice Response

» Make changes by touch-tone phone

» Can also review information

» Employees are also often able to automatically retrieve documents by fax

» Does not provide a method to make "text" changes

Internet and Intranets

Access via PC enables employees from different locations to access, share, retrieve, and update information.

Using the Internet hastens the move to paperless payroll and HR administration while at the same time increasing communication to employees.

Besides the investment in developing a secure corporate Web site or company intranet and the employee self-service applications themselves, organizations may need to make a significant investment to provide each employee with a Windows-based PC running Web browser software, plus training on the new technology.

Managers benefit from self-service too

Self-service applications allow managers to see data when and how they want to see it, cutting down the time they need to review information and make decisions.

Self-service through an outsourcing company—the ASP model

Under this type of arrangement, the employer is not required to maintain an expensive in-house system to support self-service.

The ASP itself hosts each application at its location

Implementing Internet Technology

Build a project management team

Select hardware and software

» Client software—which web browser to use;

» Server software—which web server to use;

» Type of TCP/IP (Transfer Control Protocol/ Internet Protocol) connection—enables data to be transferred from one computer to another;

» Modem speed—determines how fast information is transmitted; and

»How to coordinate the use of the Internet
with the payroll/HRMS database.

Encourage use of the technology

The approach should be simplistic and user-friendly: an easy-to-navigate site that is geared to the employee with the least computer skills.

Training of employees is necessary as a way of encouraging use.

Address security concerns

Develop appropriate policies on Internet codes of conduct

»The policies should also address copyright issues

Web-Enabled Applications

A Web-enabled application is one that uses the Internet as another means of accessing an organization's data and the HRMS application logic itself.

Web-enabled applications promote employee self-service by allowing internal users to access and act on the information they need when and where it is convenient for them.

How Web-enablement works.

The two most important elements of Web-enabled applications are:

»Accessing the data, and

»Accessing the application logic behind the data, which allows data changes to be validated and processed. *(Access to the application logic is important to keep employers from having to rewrite the logic specifically for the Web-enabled application.)*

»Elements needed for Web-enablement.

–Internet infrastructure to allow large numbers
of users to gain secure access easily

–Web-enabling tools

–Core technology expertise

–HRMS application expertise

–Design and media skills

–Workflow strategy

CHAPTER 13

Managements Styles

Basic Management Theory

Management/supervisory duties differ from the duties the manager performed before becoming a member of management. Payroll managers typically are responsible for planning, staffing, training, evaluating, counseling, delegating, reporting etc. The production work is generally done by other payroll department staff members.

Two types of management theories were reviewed.

Situational leadership
Developed by Paul Hershey and Ken Blanchard

» Task behavior (guidance)—Managers who like to exercise control over their employees including controlling communication, work procedures and organization

» Relationship behavior (support)—Managers who place few restrictions on their employees and seek their support and friendship. Employees are encouraged to accept responsibility and reach their full potential

» Combinations of the two types of leadership also exist:

  – Low Task/high relationship—Managers who seek mutual trust and support with little control sought

  – High Task/high relationship—Managers who like to control the job and procedures while attempting to coach employees to their full potential and encourage open lines of communication

-Low Task/low relationship—Managers who delegate many jobs and who prefer little personal contact with their employees

-High Task/low relationship—Managers who like to control their and direct employees performance but who want little feedback or communication with their staff

-In situational leadership managers are encourage to develop the appropriate combination of leadership skills needed by their payroll environment.

Principle-centered leadership
Developed by Stephen Covey

» There are four parts of this leadership style which form the basis of an organizations strength

-Security—Knowing our strengths and maintaining self-esteem. Do you know your job? Accuracy rates? Customer service?

-Guidance—The direction on which we base our decisions and actions. Guidance derived from integrity, honesty, and fairness will result in equity.

-Wisdom—Maintaining balance between all areas effecting payroll. An example would be taking information and using it to ensure competence and effectiveness in the department

-Power—The energy to decide, to act and to change. Accomplishing the task at hand regardless of the circumstances internally or externally facing you.

» The "Golden Rule" is the backbone of principle-centered leadership. Treat others as you want to be treated. Involve all employees in your goals and objectives for the department.

Empowerment

Giving employees the tools necessary to obtain their objectives. The key is to have employees take ownership of a task, allowing them to be motivated and to derive satisfaction for completing the task and accomplishing their objective.

Five steps to empowerment:
>»Establish the desired results

>»Provide guidance

>»Identify resources available to accomplish the task

>»Hold people accountable

>»Identify consequences

Management Skills

Some fundamental skills needed to manage are: strategic planning/organizing, giving directions, controlling progress, and upward communication with management.

Providing quality products to customers is a key objective to any business. The payroll department needs to provide quality service to its employees, management, outside vendors and taxing authorities.

Strategic Planning and Organizing

The starting point for any task is the formation of a strategic plan for the task and to organize the employees and resources to complete the task in the desired fashion.

>»Define goals and objectives

>»Define the time frame

>»Define all subtasks

>–Break down the overall project into small pieces each
with their own time frame for completion.

>»Analyze available resources

>–Employees, equipment, budget, information,
internal and external suggestions.

>»Evaluate Costs

Staffing

Hiring the right employee is one of the most important decisions a manager can make.

>»Prehiring analysis—Do we need additional staff? Should
the structure of the payroll department be changed?

»Job Descriptions—Use as a hiring tool initially and a means of measuring job performance once the individual is hired. The job description should list the duties and responsibilities of the position as well as technical skills and performance skills needed to successfully fill the position.

–Educational requirements

–Basic job knowledge

–Training opportunities

–Supervisory duties and skills

–Communication and interactive skills needed

Keep It Legal

Be sure all qualifications for the job are job-related and all duties and responsibilities listed make up the essential functions of the job.

Recruiting

Internal applicants may be familiar with the organization and the manager has access to past performance evaluations. Outside applicants may possess skills not found in any internal candidate but may come at a higher overall cost.

»Interviewing

–Seek evidence of the technical and performance skills identified in the job description. Ask each applicant the same questions so no preference is shown to any one applicant. Be sure to ask open-ended questions.

»Delegating

– All successful payroll managers must learn to delegate tasks and responsibility. Failure to do so will ensure a speedy burn out for the manager and unhappy employees.

–Assign responsibility—Be sure to tell the employee the full expectations of the task.

–Hold onto accountability

–Strike a balance

»Training

–This can be used to improve skills and knowledge but may not improve an employee's attitude. All training should be aimed at improving the skills and knowledge needed to achieve the department's mission.

–Classroom training

–Giving feedback

–Coaching

–Demonstrations

–Setting goals

Directing Employees

The manager is responsible for directing their employees to work towards obtaining the department's goals and objectives. There are four skills the manager must employ in order to accomplish this task: listening, providing feedback, coaching and leading.

Listening

We retain only 25% of what we hear eight hours after we hear what we heard. Enhance your listening skills by using "reflective listening" which is a device in which you repeat what you thought you heard the individual say.

Barriers to listening

» Distractions from phone calls, people walking into your office, similar interruptions

» Tuning out the speaker

» Reacting emotionally rather than rationally

» Failing to listen to the speaker's body language

» Not meaning what you say

» Thinking ahead about your response rather than listening to the speaker

Countermeasures to barriers

» Have your phone calls answered, close your office door, avoid interruptions

» Focus on what the speaker is saying; do not anticipate your response

» Maintain eye contact with the speaker

Providing feedback

» Advise the employee of the performance expected of them and tell them if they have achieved the goals established for them.

» Rewards reinforce and encourage positive behavior; punishment encourages modification.

»Focus on the behaviors, what is expected and not expected of the employee, not your like or dislike of the individual

»Keep feedback current

»Be specific, don't generalize

»Praise publicly, punish privately

Coaching

This helps improve the knowledge and skills employees need to perform their jobs.

»Orientation and training of new employees

»Teaching new job skills

»Explaining departmental policies and procedures

Counseling

Used by managers to help an employee resolve personal problems or attitudes adversely effecting job performance. Managers must use effective feedback and listening skills when utilizing this technique. Counseling may be necessary in the following situations:

»After corporate reorganizations, mergers or acquisitions

»After downsizing

»When salaries have been frozen or salary increases eliminated

»When conflicts between employees arise

»When employees feel unappreciated, burned out or overworked

»When an employee is affected on the job by non-work circumstances

Leadership

Whereas coaching and counseling are generally conducted by the manager on a one on one basis with an employee, leadership must be provided by the manager to the entire department.

»Have a vision—Share with employees where the department is headed and the mission of the department. Employees must know how this meshes with the overall vision and mission of the organization as a whole.

»Building team support—Create an atmosphere where employees are treated fairly and feel like they are important to you and the organization.

»Seek partners—Managers need to support each
    other throughout the organization

»Lead by example

Controlling Performance

When the manager sees that an employee's performance is lacking and
that the department's goals and objectives are not being met measures to
correct the situation must occur. Managers must find ways to **motivate** their
employees to attempt to guide them on the path desired by the organization.
What motivates one employee may not motivate another. Managers must try
to find what motives each of his employees individually; money is not always
the answer.

»Control to improve performance—Use periodic
    evaluations, system edits, verification of work, external
    audits, internal controls and documentation.

»Provide alternatives to money—Achievement,
    leadership, affiliation, recognition

Reporting

Besides guiding one's department to achieve personal and departmental
success the manager is also responsible for upward communication with his/
her superiors.

Progress reports, physical and verbal, may be necessary to convince upper
management of departmental success.

»Statistical reports

»Legislative updates

»Be sure reports are concise, clear and necessary

Conducting and Attending Meetings

»Plan according to the type of meeting

–Is the meeting informational? Will a decision
    or decisions be made as a result of this
    meeting? Will there be brainstorming?

»Prepare accordingly

–Consider the order of the meeting and provide
    attendees with appropriate agendas.

»Keep the meeting on track

»Encourage participation

–Ask open ended questions

»Keep minutes of the meeting

Keep Written Policies and Procedures

Documentation is a way to ensure uniformity, simplify training and provide a reference tool for new employees.

»Company policies

–Vacation, benefits, termination etc.

»Departmental procedures

»Disaster recovery plans

»System user manuals

»Job descriptions

Crisis Management

The ability to prevent and control a crisis is one of the manager's most important duties. The manager needs to have a plan of action in place should a crisis occur.

Preventing a crisis
Be proactive

»Create a crisis prevention team

»Plan for the "worst case scenario"

»Be sure all systems have "back-ups"

»Maintain open communications so potential problems can be circumvented

»Cross train personnel

»Regularly review departmental policies, procedures and documentation

»Be sure your department is flexible enough to handle any crisis should it arise

Managing or controlling a crisis
Manage a crisis so that the least of amount of departmental damage results.

»Maintain calm

»Isolate the crisis

»Confront the problem at hand

»Analyze potential solutions for the situation

»Keep department members informed of the
situation and attempted solution

»Document the plan you are enacting and the
consequences resulting from this plan

»Express appreciation to all who assisted in circumventing the crisis

After the crisis
Lessons to be learned—learn from the situation that resulted.

»Conduct a team meeting and discuss the
results of the corrective measure.

»Take measures to prevent similar problems from happening.

»List successful results of plan enacted.

»Be sure all appropriate personnel were recognized for their efforts.

Extracting positives from the crisis

»Meet with upper management to discuss
the crisis and the outcome.

»Network with others to see how they may
have handled a similar situation.

»Review the stress levels of staff members
resulting from this situation.

»Follow through on all modifications to your
original crisis intervention.

»Build on team spirit.

Time Management

Prioritizing is up to the manager—Classify duties

»Urgent and important—needs immediate attention

»Not urgent but important—can be done later

»Urgent but not important—pressing activities
that may be easy to accomplish

»Not urgent and not important—time wasting activities

Scheduling and delegating—keys to time management—Schedule activities keeping in mind the goals of the department and organization as a whole. Delegate duties and encourage ownership of the task by also delegating responsibility and authority on the employee. Be sure to provide the employee with all the resources needed to successfully complete the delegated task.

Team Building

Team building can increase productivity, reduce costs, make more effective use of available resources and solve problems easier by using brainstorming techniques and member talents.

Characteristics of a successful team
Define specific goals and objectives, assign roles, brainstorming, agree to disagree, maintain open communication, blame no one for mistakes.

Managing different employee styles
Contributors, collaborators, communicators, challengers.

Performance Evaluations
Performance evaluations provide a formal, written record of how employees are performing relative to preset departmental and organizational goals.

» Other purposes include:

- Identifying bad performers

- Documentation for salary increases

- Promotability of employee

- Training and disciplinary needs

- Documentation should legal actions later result

» Avoid ineffective performance evaluations:

- Guilt over negative evaluations

- No management accountability

- Improper application of standards

» Effective performance evaluations:

- Objective job-related goals and performance criteria

- Managerial training in conducting evaluations

- Written guidelines in place for administering the evaluation system

- Mechanisms in place to allow employee disagreement

–Does not place unreasonable technical and
time constraints on managers

Evaluation Is An Ongoing Process

Managers should be constantly monitoring employee performance to ensure that they are on track at all times. Informal evaluations should take place throughout the year to allow the employee time to remedy any short comings he/she may have encountered.

Promoting Quality Customer Service In Payroll

Satisfying the customer should be the primary focus of all departments within an organization. Payroll's customers are its employees who expect a correct compensation each pay period. Other payroll customers are the accounting function, taxing authorities, upper management, outside vendors etc. Several goals and objective can be put into place which applies to each customer of the payroll function.

»Reliability—Dependability and accuracy

»Responsiveness

»Assurance—Accurate and courteous responses are required.

»Empathy

»Tangibles—Neat and well organized payroll
areas promote confidence.

»Customer Service—Role playing techniques, case studies

Providing Customer Service in a Shared Services Environment

A shared service involves the consolidation of related functions and integration of the processes throughout the organization. Call center's have been enacted for "one stop shopping" to provide employees with answers to payroll related questions. Web pages also have been designed to assist employees in changing personal data directly without interaction with a payroll or human resource department member. Better quality customer service Reduced error rates, increased efficiencies, economies of scale, cost containment, better customer relations, consistent use of organizational policies and procedures.

Before implementing a shared services environment the following should be considered:

Determine the need for change

Cost analysis, customer satisfaction, survey employees

Define your goals

Analyze your current processes from end-to-end

Eliminate redundancies and multiple handoffs. Prepare to deal with corporate culture issues – Resistance to change, employees may feel threatened Focus on the process rather than the function – Emphasize the implementation of the best practices. Conduct a cost/benefit analysis and a feasibility study – Measure any increased initial cost of implementation and anticipated cost savings. Determine the functions to be included – Human Resources, Payroll, Benefits, Compensation, and Accounting etc. Determine structural issues – Determine the chain of command. Will the shared services center become a separate business unit? What will the organization chart look like? Determine service delivery methods – Cross-trained generalists, internal issue experts, interactive voice response, interactive online systems

Research Needs

The payroll manager should stay abreast of the latest tax laws and amendments, employment-related issues and know all policies and issues the organization has in place which effect payroll.

Tracking Tax Laws and Regulations

The backbone of all federal tax requirements revolve around the Internal Revenue Code (IRC) and the Internal Revenue Service Regulations (IRS). The Internal Revenue Code contains the tax laws passed by Congress and signed by the President. The IRS regulations are interpretations of the law developed by the IRS and approved by the U.S. Treasury Department that are designed to help taxpayers comply with the laws. Internal Revenue Code comprises Title 26 of the U.S. Code a compilation of all federal taxes – Ex. IRC 217 AKA 26 USC 217. IRS regulations can be found in Title 26 of the Code of Federal Regulations, which contains all federal agency regulations interpreting federal laws. Previously referred to by Public Law number – P.L. 105-206

» SSA Web Site

–www.ssa.gov State Government Resources – Different publications for each state. Non-governmental Resources – Various private publishers provide resources for use in interpreting state and federal tax regulations.

Employment Laws and Regulations

Wage-hour, garnishment, child support, immigration, anti-discrimination, family leave etc. also effect the processing of a payroll.

Company Policies and Procedures

Policy and procedural manuals are only effective if they are kept up to date. Be sure all staff members are notified of all changes and their effective dates.

Union Contracts

The private sector now has only 13.9% union representation while the public sector has a 37.5% union representation. Watch for dues check offs, fringe benefit contributions, upcoming layoffs, wages increases, probationary employees, overtime/premium pay provisions of all union contracts. Be sure you understand the contract in effect and are able to easily identify all union members. Specific reports may be required by the union and your organization regarding union dues and membership. Keep all contracts up to date.